# THE WHITE WORKING CLASS

## WHAT EVERYONE NEEDS TO KNOW®

# THE WHITE WORKING CLASS

## WHAT EVERYONE NEEDS TO KNOW®

### JUSTIN GEST

OXFORD

UNIVERSITY PRESS

# OXFORD
UNIVERSITY PRESS

Oxford University Press is a department of the University of Oxford. It furthers
the University's objective of excellence in research, scholarship, and education
by publishing worldwide. Oxford is a registered trade mark of Oxford University
Press in the UK and certain other countries.

"What Everyone Needs to Know" is a registered trademark
of Oxford University Press.

Published in the United States of America by Oxford University Press
198 Madison Avenue, New York, NY 10016, United States of America.

Library of Congress Cataloging-in-Publication Data
Names: Gest, Justin, author.
Title: The white working class : what everyone needs to know / Justin Gest.
Description: New York, NY : Oxford University Press, [2018] |
Series: What everyone needs to know | Includes bibliographical references and index.
Identifiers: LCCN 2017051420 (print) | LCCN 2017055633 (ebook) |
ISBN 9780190861421 (Updf) | ISBN 9780190861438 (Epub) |
ISBN 9780190861407 (pbk. : alk. paper) | ISBN 9780190861414 (hardcover : alk. paper)
Subjects: LCSH: Whites—United States—Social conditions. |
Whites—Great Britain—Social conditions. | Working class—United States—
Social conditions. | Working class—Great Britain—Social conditions.
Classification: LCC E184.A1 (ebook) | LCC E184.A1 G424 2018 (print) |
DDC 305.809—dc23
LC record available at https://lccn.loc.gov/2017051420

# CONTENTS

# PREFACE

In recent years, a populist wave has raised the profile of "white working-class" people in North America and Europe. Radical Right parties scored victories across European Union states, Britain voted to leave the European Union, and the United States elected President Donald Trump to enact a nationalist, protectionist "America First" agenda.

Each of these political movements claimed it would seize government from wealthy, cosmopolitan elites and return it to the masses—a rebuke of a transnational public sphere and globalized economy that has increased inequality, fostered greater migration, blurred traditional cultural distinctions, and widened the gap between those who live in capitals and those in the countryside. Behind much of this revolt is the white working class.

This populist wave consolidated a sense of identity and power among citizens who have felt voiceless for decades despite their historically privileged social position. In the mid-twentieth century, white people without university degrees comprised the vast majority of populations in the United States and Europe. Though their status was not overtly acknowledged or visible, they were a political powerhouse and bellwether. Bolstered by their numbers and organized by large trade unions, white working-class people constituted an integral part of the political center—the most sought-after constituencies in politics and markets.

However, during the 1970s and early 1980s, the manufacturing economy declined and gave rise to one defined by high technology and a global race for talent. Swiftly, as factories shuttered and labor markets grew more competitive, white working-class lives became characterized by less money, less stability, and less political clout. This constituency—diminished, but still great in number—became an anachronism that was derided as lazy, bigoted, and simple. Many continued to vote for center-Left parties, but remained relatively sidelined and frustrated for decades until the recent populist wave harvested their anger and generated a string of shocking electoral triumphs.

Nevertheless, the public understanding of the "white working class" remains vaguely defined; they are more of a specter in the collective mind than a well-comprehended constituency. Who are white working-class people? What do they believe? What has driven them to break so sharply with the world's seeming trajectory toward a borderless, interconnected meritocracy? What is the basis for their attitudes and behavior? How can a group with such enduring power feel marginalized? What does their future hold?

In this book, I will offer an overview of this perplexing population group that must be understood if the world is to adapt to the social and political phenomena they are driving. While I will focus on trends in the United States and the United Kingdom—the sites of two pivotal political developments, Brexit and the election of Donald Trump—I will also connect these events to broader trends. I propose a set of essential questions that drive much of the political debate, and then address each one by providing context and summarizing in plain language the most advanced descriptive and explanatory social scientific research available. The book's sections move from introducing this constituency, to understanding their identity, to clarifying their public attitudes, to explaining their electoral behavior, to finally addressing public debates and their future prospects. The content is derived principally from my own field research in the postindustrial regions of Youngstown, Ohio, and East London, England; summaries of the top scholarship addressing this subject matter; and extensive, fresh data analysis tailored to the purposes of this book. In the end, I hope you, the reader, will have a more nuanced grasp of a complicated constituency at the center of transatlantic social and political controversy.

# ACKNOWLEDGMENTS

This book began on November 9, 2016, the day after Donald Trump was elected president of the United States of America. My editors at Oxford University Press, Niko Pfund and Angela Chnapko, had just published my monograph, *The New Minority: White Working Class Politics in an Age of Immigration and Inequality*, and there was a suddenly voracious appetite for content about white working-class people—the constituency thought to have tilted the electoral scales in favor of Donald Trump in the United States and Brexit in the United Kingdom. While *The New Minority* did not predict these events, it is one of the few pieces of research that rigorously examined this underestimated, perplexing group in the preceding years.

That same day, my colleagues at George Mason University asked me to change the subject of a previously scheduled research presentation to address the election results. It was informally entitled "What the Hell Just Happened?" Speaking to a packed seminar room made me realize that there was enormous confusion among political scientists and members of the public alike. While observers scrambled to read memoirs and commentary about white working-class people, it became clear that there were many pressing questions and very little research written in an accessible manner. My senior colleague and mentor, Jack Goldstone, was quick to encourage me to address this void. The thoughtful, provocative questions raised by my faculty colleagues and in countless conversations and presentations thereafter informed several of those addressed in the chapters that follow.

In preparing this book on a tight turnaround, I was aided by a number of generous colleagues and superb research assistants. Tyler Reny, an excellent statistician and brilliant thinker in his own right, helped prepare the data analysis. Aaron Roper and Sheyda Aboii helped compile some of the book's secondary source research with their characteristic diligence and care. Eve Fairbanks, Rob Ford, and Pete Mohanty offered wonderfully helpful reviews for Oxford University Press, each of which improved the book substantially. I am also grateful to Shalini Balakrishnan, Alexcee Bechthold, and again Angela Chnapko at Oxford University Press for their assistance with copyediting and early reviews of my work.

I would also like to thank my friends and family members—my parents, Max and Gail, my brother and sister-in-law, Darren and Rebecca, my nephew Phillip—for supporting me. Special thanks to Monika and Valentina, who roll with each new project I tackle and make me feel so good about each one I pursue.

One question unanswered by the body of this book is how I—an immigration scholar, born and raised in Los Angeles—became interested in the phenomena associated with white working-class politics. My earliest and most intimate acquaintance came from my near daily interactions with my beloved grandfather, Alvin Litt. Born in Brooklyn to parents of Russian Jewish heritage, he served in the United States Navy at the end of the Second World War, and then dropped out of university to marry my grandmother, Jeannette, and open a modest department store in her rural hometown of Fitzgerald, Georgia. In many ways, their lives mirrored the greater struggle for white working-class people after the 1960s. They left an idyllic Southern town to pursue bigger things in a rapidly urbanizing, globalizing Los Angeles, but ultimately struggled with the big city's anonymity and open market. They yearned for the simplicity of earlier times and the stability of past relationships. As the children of immigrants, they embraced newcomers but were also frustrated by the way they altered the society they once knew. They were simultaneously characterized by love and resentment, dignity and disorientation. They had an appreciation for the good life even if they often had a hard time recognizing how good they had it. They were complicated, and I loved them very much. They both died during the course of my research on white working-class politics, but I like to think they would be proud of the work they helped inspire.

# 1

# INTRODUCTION AND DEFINITIONS

## *What does it mean to be "white"?*

"Race" is a man-made concept that gives social meaning to the shade of one's skin. There is no biological basis or scientific definition for being "white"—it is only part of a gradient of skin pigmentation. However, the associations with "white" skin and the supposed boundaries that define who qualifies as "white" hold great power and influence over the way we understand and interact with one another. Consequently, our discussion about the "white working class" must begin with a brief history and discussion of how this fundamental social construction has led to grave social implications over time.

The term "white" arose from contact between European explorers, traders, and settlers who came in contact with indigenous people whom they classified as non-white.[1] With myths about inferiority and savagery of indigenous peoples, whiteness was used to rationalize the dispossession of people's land and the exploitation of their resources.

Despite Europeans' historical enslavement by Vikings and North Africans, blackness would soon be associated with bondage, and whiteness with freedom.[2] Quickly, race became a fundamental principle of a system that served the interests of the powerful and subordinated others.[3]

Anthropologists began using the term "white" in the mid- to late 1700s, as a classification based on physical features and complexion. Early on, whiteness was associated with purity and even female beauty.[4] In the 1770s, the Dutch anthropologist Petrus Camper drew a chart of faces and skulls that placed black faces next to apes and the European faces closer to the Greek God ideal. While Camper was actually an advocate of human equality, this diagram became a central component of a pseudo-scientific racist worldview, irrefutable proof to its supporters of white supremacy.[5]

This myth of supremacy would justify the African slave trade and the colonization of the Global South for centuries. However, it would also placate exploited white laborers; while they were not slaves, their mobility was constrained by rigid class hierarchies in the same manner, and they were capable of rebellion. W. E. B. Du Bois explained how white supremacy offered some psychological compensation to these alienated white workers. In lieu of economic opportunity, white laborers were given "public deference" and "titles of courtesy." The police were drawn from their ranks, and the courts, dependent on their votes, treated them with leniency.[6]

For subsequent generations in the United States, whiteness endured as a refuge from association with black slaves. White servants and black slaves were often described in the same terms.[7] Both were called "shiftless," "irresponsible," "unfaithful," "ungrateful," and "dishonest." The English reformer William Cobbett once claimed that white workers in English factories were "slaves" under more strenuous conditions than those of the West Indies.[8] This broadbrushing prompted white people to pursue an ethnoracial—rather than class-based—identity. To mark this distinction, whiteness became institutionalized in legal systems.[9]

Throughout the late eighteenth, nineteenth, and early twentieth centuries, being white was key to citizenship, assimilation, and social mobility. In 1790, the American Congress restricted naturalization to white people. And over the next century and a half, courts were tasked with deciding who was white and why they were white.[10] Accordingly, every new wave of immigrants— each different in some new way—sought designation as "white" to secure the advantages afforded to such qualified individuals in the United States.[11] For these new arrivals, becoming white meant that they could pursue their lives freely outside of the color line that kept black Americans a permanent underclass. It also meant that they had wider access to the levers of power and participation. In the British Empire, race was considered alongside class status and rank in considerations of inclusion and exclusion.

While the explicit institution of race in law and public procedure has since been largely removed in North America and Europe, race continues to structure our lives in countless, subtle ways. Issues like voter suppression, immigration, and prison sentencing all feature racial undertones. More informally, white people enjoy the benefits of being the default human being. Richard Dyer put it succinctly: "Other people are raced; we are just people."[12] And, consequently, across nearly every indicator, white people have greater wealth, higher incomes, better educational opportunities, access to better health care, more representation in government, and lower rates of incarceration. The list goes on.

Today, white people in North America and Europe continue to define themselves in opposition to non-whites— whether black or Muslim, Latino or Asian. Whiteness remains a necessary corollary to non-white status, rather than a race in and of itself. Working-class whites tend to organize around their whiteness because they often lack a job that provides a stable, distinctive identity and want to associate themselves with upper-class whites.[13] The last half-century has seen an extraordinary decline in the pay and social status associated with the trades and professions that white working-class people pursue, along with the unions that protected their status and interests. So while middle-class white people can identify with achieved social statuses and therefore invest less in ethnic and racial distinctions, white working-class people cannot.[14]

Although white people remain able to define who isn't white, they have increasing difficulty defining who is. This is a product of compounding factors. To start, whiteness is an increasingly amorphous idea. It was once thought that the British white working class never needed to define itself.[15] Similarly, in the United States, assimilation of immigrants followed a trajectory of "Anglo-conformity" where newcomers were expected to accumulate the attributes of "WASPdom" to ultimately become Americans.[16] However, British and Anglo-American identity has evolved with the incorporation of alternative "white" identities derived from France, Ireland, Germany, and Scandinavia in Britain, but also Hungarians, Iberians, Slavs, Italians, Greeks, Jews, Arabs, and European-origin Latinos in the United States. So whiteness is now an amalgam of ethnicities.

This internal diversity not only reduces the coherency of white norms and culture; its inconsistent boundaries also, over time, weaken the sense that white people form a group. Intermarriage among different ethnic groups further entangles their various cultural lineages such that whiteness is most generally characterized—at best—by its necessary diversity, and—at worst—by a cultural malaise and a tenuous yet critical grip on power. In other words, whiteness now, more than ever, is created in response to a sense of threat not only against white livelihoods but against the cultural goods of "Western civilization" and the very foundations of the modern world itself. White people feel this threat to different extents: Younger, middle class, university graduates tend to reject it, which reinforces the links between white identity and marginality. To identify a stronger sense of groupness, these upwardly mobile white people have sought out subcultures related to other identities like ideology, lifestyle, or sexuality. Whiteness may now legitimately signify so many things that it ceases to mean anything in particular.

When they are meaningful, political claims by white people—when made as white people—have become unpalatable. There are a number of reasons why. A sense of white consciousness is precisely what led to the systemic oppression and suppression of ethnic minorities over the course of time. Consequently, it is difficult to construe any advancement of the interests of white people as "white people" without concern that this necessarily relegates the interests of other constituencies that were historically disadvantaged. Indeed, since the 1960s, the only groups that have explicitly sought the advancement of white people as "white people" have been white supremacists. Accordingly, public officials and civil society groups have been wary of adopting any cause limited to the advancement of white people as "white people." Aside from likely allegations of bigotry, any such efforts would also be challenged by critics questioning the moral or even practical justification for specifically aiding a group subject to so much historical advantage.

Consequently, many white working-class people feel that white identity—once and still a complicated symbol of supremacy—is now out of bounds.

### What does it mean to be "working class"?

"Working class" is a European term that distinguished a landed aristocracy (later also owners of capital) and religious clergy from those who literally had to work for a living. The working classes encompassed everyone who sold their labor and skills for wages—whether this work was white collar, blue collar, physical, creative, or cognitive. In Karl Marx's terms, working-class people were the "proletariat" who did not own the means of production. However, with the decline and mechanization of manufacturing economies in Europe and North America, a substantial middle class of managers, professionals, and highly skilled technicians emerged.

While they did not own the means of production, they profited from them and lived distinct lives from laborers pursuing manual labor and basic services. They joined growing numbers of public sector employees subject to state ownership and service employees who employ alternative means of production and increasingly work remotely. These trends have both complicated the originally simple class hierarchy and eroded the ranks of the working class.

There are multiple ways to identify a working-class person. A simple metric looks at people's income. Income is straightforward to measure, and it is measured widely. However, while it is universally thought that working-class people earn less than credentialed professionals and owners of capital, the threshold is not obvious. Where should the income line be drawn? Should the poor be lumped in with the working class or set apart? Should income be defined in absolute or relative terms? Living standards, inflation, and social circumstances in different time periods also make comparison difficult.[17]

Another way to identify the working class focuses on the nature of their occupations. However, industrial decline has blurred the link between occupation and working-class identity. As call centers, hospitals, rideshares, and other service jobs replace industrial jobs, it is increasingly difficult to solely rely on historic associations.[18] Today, one might ask: Do you work with your hands? Do you wear a uniform? Is your labor routinized? Are you on an hourly wage or salary? An affirmative answer to any of these suggests a working-class life, but not necessarily. Surgeons work with their hands. Airplane pilots wear uniforms. Some engineers' work is routinized. Independent consultants are paid hourly. The occupation-based definition can also miss people in a growing informal economy.[19]

Perhaps the most valid and reliable way to identify working-class people is by accounting for their educational attainment.[20] Analyses often use education levels as a proxy for skill set or human capital, key factors in determining what kind of work an individual can obtain.[21] Still, there are many exceptions. What about unemployed university graduates with massive debt? What about dot-com and mobile app millionaires who were university dropouts? High-earning tradespeople, designers, and craftspeople? People with university degrees who pursue low-paying jobs? It is noteworthy that these are less common profiles, but they reveal exceptions that confound attempts to authoritatively define the working class.

More problematically, class is—at its core—a social concept as much as an economic concept. Income, occupation, and education ignore the social and cultural implications of certain careers and backgrounds. A number of researchers have turned to culture- or religion-based definitions of the working class.[22] While these definitions present a different perspective on working-class identities and pertain to taste, norms, region, and lifestyle, they are often subjective, variously categorized in surveys, and difficult to generalize across a population. There is also the risk of stereotyping and imposing judgment on the population under study.[23] The way we define the working class impacts the conclusions we may draw from the data available. Better approaches can use blended definitions combining income, occupational, educational, and cultural criteria to identify the working class. However, very few sources collect all such data, and problems with boundaries and exceptions persist. In my previous research, I let the people I met define for themselves if they were working class, but I also used more objective markers. In this book, I assign working-class status to people who did not complete university degrees. While this is flawed for the reasons I acknowledge above, education credentials are widely measured and a relatively reliable predictor of people's income, professional rank, and accompanying cultural differences.

It is worth underscoring that such definitional choices can significantly affect the results of an analysis. For example, a white working-class person who identifies his or her status by income tends to be slightly more liberal-leaning than one who defines his or her status according to his or her education. Analyzing data from the American National Election Studies (ANES), white working-class individuals—defined as those in the bottom third of incomes—are more likely to identify as Democrats, more sympathetic to the Democratic Party, less sympathetic to the Republican Party, more liberal, more likely to vote for a Democratic president, and more supportive of welfare recipients and "illegal aliens" than those defined in terms of education levels.[24] In any statistical analysis presented in this book, I clarify what definition is employed. While this is sometimes a subjective decision, in many cases, it is a product of what data are available or most reliable.

The difficulty in identifying "working-class" people has undermined working-class consciousness, as much as it has undermined the generalizability of social scientific research. In being defined in so many crosscutting ways, "working class"—like "white"—is a somewhat amorphous, conflicted identity. In this light, one of the greatest historical—even if dubious—achievements of the recent wave of Radical Right populism in the United States and Europe has been to foster a sense of cohesion among an otherwise dispersed, complex constituency of people and to reinvigorate class- and race-based identity.

### How do these understandings change across countries?

#### United Kingdom

In Britain, class identity is a complex source of pride and limitation. Britons see class as an inherited trait and therefore a matter of entitlement and birthright. It is signaled by factors like geographic origin, accent, and perhaps even appearance. A 31-year-old news editor I interviewed in Dagenham said, "You never class yourself as anything other than working class. You can keep whatever company you like, and have as much money as you'd like, but you'll always be a product of your working-class roots . . . a working-class boy done good." The idea that class identity is static throughout time and regardless of personal mobility is a product of people's comfort with their identity, but also the endurance of the stereotypes imposed by others.

In discussing their social position in British society, white working-class people intertwine their social affinities with the sense of rejection by others in superior classes. This self-awareness has produced a sort of reluctant reverence for those above them, but also complacency in their own status.[25] British workers take pride in being ordinary, authentic individuals because it is what distinguishes them from the middle and upper classes, who act out of social motives rather than naturally.

A 25-year-old who works for his father's flooring business in Barking told me, "Even if I got really rich, I'd still have a working-class mentality. I'd have a nice car and all that, but the people I get along with are here. I can't get along with people from [upscale] Chelsea. They look down on people who speak like us East End Cockneys. My mate from here started a job in Chelsea, and they are quite stuck up with him over there with all of his 'Allo Darlin!' I think that if I went for the same job against someone from Chelsea, they would get it because of the way I speak and the way I look. They wouldn't wear tracksuit bottoms. You're labeled a 'chav.'"

"Chav" is a pejorative label for white working-class individuals in Britain. The stereotypical characteristics of chavs include belligerence, stupidity, and an affinity for low-brow culture.[26] Though they are subject to such derogatory labeling, white working-class people consciously separate themselves from a would-be underclass of white people without the dignity of employment, morality, and self-discipline: those who would instead be characterized as benefit-dependent, criminal, or addicted to alcohol or narcotics. This sense of superiority has given white working-class people a sense of social position—beneath some but above others—for centuries. It has contributed to the sentiment that Britain's white working-class people, with all their flaws, are central to British society—that there is dignity in their struggle, authenticity in their roots, moral virtue in their culture, and an exclusivity that upwardly mobile minorities cannot access. This has informed a sense of class pride and solidarity that has pervaded social relations since the 1930s.

There are several historical explanations for this sense of class pride and solidarity in Britain. E. P. Thompson famously traced the contemporary working-class identity back to the eighteenth century, when ideological and structural changes brought about by the French and Industrial Revolutions caused British workers to become class conscious.[27] Others related white British working-class consciousness to the preindustrial world, a two-class society that pitted a poor, occupationally diverse group of servants against a prevailing class of elites.[28] Reflecting on his time in England, Marx himself argued that the aristocracy fomented popular hatred for Irish workers among the English working class to prevent the two oppressed groups from uniting. By perceiving the Irish as competitors, English workers found themselves more subject to manipulation by the landed aristocracy.

Given this unique history and heritage-based solidarity, white working-class people in Britain have been reluctant to admit immigrants of foreign origins to what is clearly a cultural—even while ostensibly class-based—fellowship. This is the case regardless of immigrant tours of service and sacrifice to the United Kingdom's military and decades of contributions to the welfare state. The British white working class tend to view immigrants as ethnically, linguistically, religiously, and culturally distinct. Many immigrants are not even of humble origins, as Britain's service sector is increasingly a home for well-educated people from Eastern and Southern Europe and beyond.

## United States

In the United States, people view class as a temporary state in a dynamic economy, despite the overwhelming evidence of immobility. The American Dream is thought to offer an equal opportunity for all, to reward hard work with upward mobility, and to give individuals agency over the direction of their lives. Accordingly, white working-class people understand their lower-status position as the product of an American meritocracy.

Many people bend their interpretation of the American Dream to reflect their own experience. The hopeful may work for companies on flexible contracts and earn incomes that offer little long-term stability and qualify them for few public benefits. Many are one misfortune away from a life of poverty and can do little to ensure that their children's future is not predestined to follow a similar, if not worse, course. Despite weighty evidence to the contrary, many insist that the American Dream exists or that hard work pays off. Forty percent of Americans consider it common for a person born to a poor family to work their way up the economic ladder.[29] Fifty-four percent of Americans believe they will be better off in ten years.[30] The American Dream is an ever-present actuality that exists independent of government regulation, standards, and popular mobilization. Capitalism gives, and capitalism can take away.

As measures of mobility drop from generation to generation and the American economy is characterized by wider inequality, the American Dream is increasingly a matter of faith. The United States is now developing a class of people who effectively inherit poverty or working-class status. According to recent Organisation for Economic Co-operation and Development (OECD) statistics, the US Gini coefficient—a score of inequality—has increased from 0.316 in the 1970s to 0.357 in the 2000s, which makes America one of the most unequal developed countries in the world. Recent studies also reveal levels of economic mobility that are much lower than people's perception. Seventy percent of Americans who are raised in the two lowest income quintiles never make it to the middle quintile.[31]

In my research and that of others, white working-class people have been unlikely to identify structural reasons for their immobility.[32] Indeed, many blame themselves. One of my respondents was a 46-year-old man who worked as a foreman at a window factory for 24 years, but was laid off in 2008. Now a laborer in a smaller metal shop, he has a nine-year-old daughter and currently lives with his parents. He said that the steel mills closed down because "the workers exploited the companies. They didn't know how good they had it. The companies gave them everything they could want, the unions, everything, until the jobs were gone. This generation will be more grateful." Like other respondents, he views companies' earlier provisions as voluntary rather than obligatory and justified.

This reflects a broader American individualism that undermines labor solidarity. Despite being tasked with protecting the interests of the working class, an Ohio Democratic Party official told me, "America is still rough and tumble, where the fittest survives. Just because I strive to get everyone a fair shot doesn't mean they get one. They still gotta try. . . . The cold reality of America is that you got to look out for yourself. You gotta work hard, have a little bit of luck, then you'll be okay. If you don't want to, then you'll be wherever your lot takes you."

But even in the best of times, the American economy was not as meritocratic as people remember. In the mid-twentieth century, unions, mafias, and political machines were engaged in cronyism, corruption, and an elaborate system of favors. And each institution was as bigoted as the manufacturers they attempted to keep in check. However, to credit such structural advantage and collusion with facilitating the stable lifestyle so many white working-class people enjoyed in the mid-twentieth century dismisses their backbreaking work and extended hours on the job, not to mention protests and collective bargaining. Americans' belief in the self-determination of the worker is akin to the entitlement with which the British have historically treated their heritage. If they cannot believe in the virtue of hard work, there is little else to believe in.

A variety of research emphasizes the deterioration of social ladders and social cohesion. Scholars point to an increasingly less progressive American tax structure,[33] the widening achievement gap between children from high- and low-income families,[34] and a growing class gap in social trust, educational achievement, and extracurricular involvement among youth.[35] Considering this growing class discrepancy, America is thought to represent more and more of "a caste system," where children inherit their social standing from their parents.[36]

Though idealized, the British (and European) system of class heritage historically locked white working-class people into their status, while the American meritocracy really only existed for white workers from an earlier era. Both markets have simply become more open to minority advancement and more difficult for all to ascend.

### What are the narratives of the white working class across time?

A key reason that white working-class people perplex observers is that multiple narratives depict their plight and attempt to explain their behavior and activities in the United States and the United Kingdom. While the first two (economic and moral narratives) are well publicized, the third narrative (health) is growing in recognition with available statistical data. While these narratives conflict with each other in numerous ways, they overlap in others and reflect a public struggle to understand, evaluate, and sometimes exonerate themselves from white working-class people's plight.

*Economic Narrative:* According to the economic narrative, the shift toward a service-oriented, high-technology, globalized economy after World War II required the outsourcing of light manufacturing and basic services to developing nations with minimal labor standards. This economic transformation undermined the social and political strength of white working-class communities by diminishing their ranks and loosening the political solidarity they possessed through organized labor and related movements. With the decline in their civic participation and clout amid new global economic pressures, states pursued neoliberal models of economics that curtailed protectionism, subsidies, and opened markets to far greater competition. The white working-class individuals who adapted to these changes have since joined globalization's winners (and losers who are at least acquiescent).

Those slower to adapt are commonly understood as the dispersed, unorganized holdouts of an earlier era without access to the benefits of a globalized economy. Over the course of the twentieth century in the United Kingdom, the proportion of the working population employed as "manual workers" fell from 75 to 38 percent, while the proportion of professionals and managers rose from 8 to 34 percent.[37] In 1940 in the United States, 74 percent of employed workers were white and did not hold professional or managerial jobs. By 2006, that percentage was 43 percent.[38] In 1940, 86 percent of adults 25 years old and over were white and without a four-year university degree. By 2007, that percentage declined to 48 percent.[39] In 1947, 86 percent of American families were white families with less than $60,000 in income (in 2005 dollars). That percentage declined to 33 percent by 2005.[40]

The postindustrial middle classes have therefore swelled with various European-origin, white communities and upwardly mobile immigrants who are integrating into a free market, capitalist system. As dual-income families, elevated life expectancies, and steady economic growth became more prevalent, university education replaced white skin as the ticket into the middle class. This transformation not only shrunk the community of those understanding themselves as white working class; it also splintered the broader working class into two groups: aspirational immigrants and poor white nationals with little mobility. The United States and the United Kingdom feature the least economic mobility among OECD countries.[41]

Parental income remains highly determinant of lifelong economic status. In the United States, mobility has stalled for over a generation.[42] (Figures 1.1 and 1.2 show how the top income terciles in the United States, and quartiles in the United Kingdom, were once occupied by a number of white people without university degrees.) This has changed dramatically over the last 50 years. In 1960, white Americans without university degrees were nearly evenly distributed across income terciles in the United States. As time went on, and even as the ranks of the middle class grew, people without university degrees joined it at a lower rate and largely fell to the bottom tier. This collapse coincided with an equally dramatic drop in union membership, first among white working-class people, and then among the population as a whole.

Advocates of this economic perspective argue that while ethnic, gender, and cultural backgrounds are factors in explaining a person's life prospects, it is the social class into which one is born that is still most determinant.[43] In this depiction, the outmoded white working class is juxtaposed with a white middle and upper class that both expanded with economic development in the twentieth century and have since created economic and cultural space between themselves and those who failed to make this socioeconomic leap. The widening gap is indeed frequently

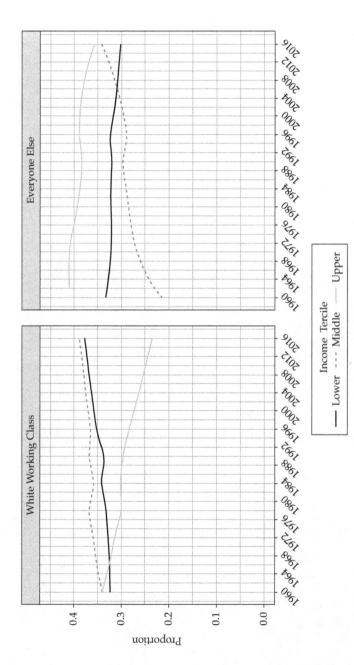

**Figure 1.1** Share of white working-class people (white people without university degrees) and all others in each income tercile in the United States, 1960–2016. Lines indicate the smoothed weighted average proportions.

*Source:* American National Election Studies cumulative file.

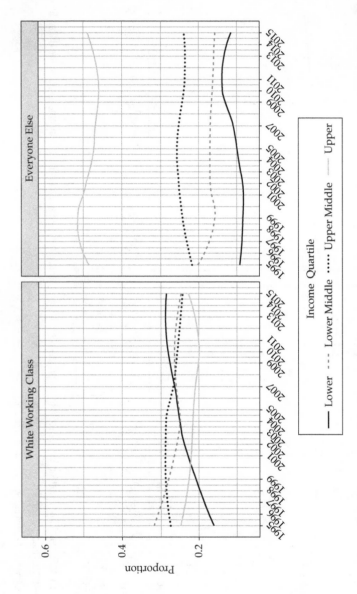

**Figure 1.2** Share of white working-class people and all others with university degrees in each income quartile in the United Kingdom, 1995–2015. Lines indicate the smoothed weighted average proportions.

*Source:* British Social Attitudes Survey.

justified on meritocratic grounds that subtly insinuate cultural differences. Nevertheless, economic explanations of white working-class marginalization argue that social stigma is merely the residue of severe inequality.

_Moral Narrative:_ A moral narrative characterizes poor white people as clinging to the unfair advantages of an earlier time, and resistant to progressive change in an effort to maintain power over minorities. The white working class is the "amoral and apolitical section in society who are neither deserving nor poor," according to Yasmin Alibhai-Brown, a British commentator. "It is a group that is against learning, anti-intellectual, and comprised of individuals who—in the words of one commentator—'despise browns and blacks' (especially if they are making something of their lives) and also education, enlightenment and internationalism."[44] Accordingly, poor white people represent an antagonist to other, often equally poor, minority groups—groups that have worked to gain equal footing through efforts like the Civil Rights Movement.

More subtly, white elites, whose parents and grandparents may have once supported policies of exclusion and rose to elite status through prejudiced systems of education and promotion, vilify poor whites.[45] In the drive to counterbalance historical discrimination, both white elites and minority groups often distance themselves from poor white people to account for their success in these systems—systems that working-class white people had a lesser hand in building. _Hillbilly Elegy_, a prominent 2016 memoir by J. D. Vance—a former Marine and Yale Law School graduate—exemplified this distancing. He described the abusive and nationalist propensities of his family members and community in rural Appalachia, which contextualized his personal ascent thanks to hard work and grandmotherly care.

In various ways, white members of the "underclass" have been singled out as behaviorally or morally inferior. In the United Kingdom, competing characterizations associate white working-class people with "backwardness" and are even thought of as "unclean" and "lazy benefit-hunting mother[s] of several children,"[46] even while white working-class people claim a rhetorical high ground as their country's "heart and soul"—the people who historically spilled blood and perspired for a continuing national existence.

In his book, *Coming Apart*, Charles Murray describes poor white people's deviant norms in the United States: "In the years after 1960, America developed something new: a white lower class that did not consist of a fringe, but of a substantial part of what was formerly the working-class population."[47] He contends that the members of this white underclass of "less-educated men" violate the traditional American norm of industriousness by claiming disability benefits, being employed in "less-than-full-time work,"[48] or leaving the workforce.[49] According to Murray, these trends cannot simply be explained away by citing macroeconomic conditions, because the overall economy grew well enough from 1960 to the present day. Instead, Murray argues that these trends are a sign that the American norm of industriousness "has softened" in the white underclass. "White males of the 2000s were less industrious than they had been twenty, thirty, or fifty years ago," he wrote, "and . . . the decay in the industriousness occurred overwhelmingly [among the least educated]."

Beyond work habits, Murray cites the deterioration of American norms with regard to religiosity and marriage. Despite the common belief that white working-class people are very religious, Murray argues that a decline in religiosity has serious implications for social mobility because of the social capital otherwise provided by churches. Similarly, Murray and others have pointed to the fact that lower-status whites are much more likely to get divorced within ten years of marriage, have children out of wedlock, and report unhappiness with their current marriage.[50] To put the scale of these trends into perspective, the extramarital birth rate among white American women with a university degree has remained nearly constant at 5 percent since the 1960s. Meanwhile, the rate of extramarital births among white American women without a high school diploma is now 60 percent.[51]

In a column lamenting white working-class support for Donald Trump's presidential candidacy, the *National Review*'s Kevin Williamson wrote,

[If] you take an honest look at the welfare dependency, the drug and alcohol addiction, the family anarchy— which is to say, the whelping of human children with all the respect and wisdom of a stray dog—you will come to an awful realization. It wasn't Beijing. It wasn't Washington, as bad as Washington can be. It wasn't immigrants from Mexico, excessive and problematic as our current immigration levels are. It wasn't any of that. Nothing happened to them. There wasn't some awful disaster. There wasn't a war or famine or a plague or a foreign occupation. Even the economic changes of the past few decades do very little to explain the dysfunction and negligence—and the incomprehensible malice—of poor white America. So the gypsum business in Garbutt ain't what it used to be. There is more to life in the 21st century than wallboard and cheap sentimentality about how the Man closed factories down.

The truth about these dysfunctional, downscale communities is that they deserve to die. Economically, they are negative assets. Morally, they are indefensible. Forget all your cheap theatrical Bruce Springsteen crap. Forget your sanctimony

about struggling Rust Belt factory towns and your
conspiracy theories about the wily Orientals stealing
our jobs. Forget your goddamned gypsum. . . . The
white American underclass is in thrall to a vicious,
selfish culture whose main products are misery and
used heroin needles.[52]

Williamson, Murray, and other commentators who have
assigned deviant norms to lower-status whites may do
so primarily to justify such people's lower social position
and distinguish establishment conservatives from their
emerging partisan bedfellows. And yet other accounts
like Vance's focus on deteriorating mores in an attempt to
signal a brewing crisis within the white working class itself. It is often difficult to distinguish between these two
agendas. Independent of the underlying objective, however, it is consequential that more attention is being paid
to the cultural norms of a white underclass,[53] in a manner
similar to the treatment of poor minority groups.

This moral account contends that white working-class
behavior is a product of cultural habits that diverge from
other groups of white people and "white culture."[54] It
juxtaposes the ostensible complacency, ignorance, and
backwardness of white working-class people with the industry, naïveté, and resourcefulness of immigrants and
minority groups, and the ingenuity and adaptations of
metropolitan elites. The ubiquity of this moral narrative
is, ironically, a barrier in itself. It hinders the advancement
of white working-class individuals, who have trouble
shaking off this stigma, and therefore improving their economic well-being and making political claims effectively.
White working-class people conventionally value hard
work and use it—for better or worse—as a mark of moral
distinction and as a means of separating themselves from
the non-white working class.

*Health Narrative*: White working-class people have always faced physical risks. In factories and mills, workers faced the possibility of being crushed, blinded, burned, or becoming a part of the very steel they curated.[55] When mills shut down and factory doors closed, communities were often left with urban blight, but also, corrupted topsoil and polluted water.[56] Although a significant number of dangerous, manual jobs have moved offshore or become automated, many of the service-sector jobs that have replaced them require repetitive motion, treacherous workplace conditions, and physical labor that still leave working-class people disproportionately exposed to health risks.

Such risks are compounded by the emotional and psychological effects of job insecurity, abandonment, isolation, and substance abuse. Reduced access to social or cultural support may relate to rising illness and death rates.[57] Since the Second World War, working class people disproportionately enlist in the military and fight in wars. Recent research suggests that there exists a hierarchy of health akin to the hierarchy of class, where those relegated to the bottom are much more likely to have poorer health.[58]

A recent analysis of life expectancies since the late 1990s suggests that these effects might have been more widely felt in the United States than in other countries.[59] Despite overall improvement in the United States, middle-aged, white, non-Hispanic individuals have experienced an increase in illness and death rates since 1998. Middle-aged, white, non-Hispanic people have also indicated key measures of distress, including "declines in self-reported health and mental health, increased reports of pain, and greater difficulties with [activities of] daily living."[60]

Since 1998, this group's mortality rate rose by half a percentage point per year. If the mortality rate had remained at its 1998 level, 96,000 deaths could have been avoided between 1999 and 2013. And if the rate had continued to decline, as it had between 1979 and 1998, by 1.8 percent per year, 488,500 deaths could have been avoided.[61] The three causes of death driving this change were suicide, drug and alcohol poisoning, and chronic liver disease or cirrhosis of the liver. Indeed, the three causes have well outpaced diabetes despite the national attention directed toward this increasingly prevalent disease. In 2011, more people died of drug and alcohol poisoning than lung cancer. Death rates for middle-aged, non-Hispanic, white individuals have actually exceeded that of their black and Hispanic peers.[62] Younger and older non-Hispanic whites also experienced similar increases in mortality but not to the same degree as the middle-aged.[63]

These increases in mortality and morbidity rates are concurrent with a growing opioid epidemic.[64] According to the Centers for Disease Control, the rate of drug overdose deaths in the United States has increased by 137 percent since 2002, while the rate of overdose deaths involving opioids (including prescription pain relievers and heroin) increased by 200 percent. In 2014, there were approximately one and a half times more deaths attributable to opioid overdoses than to motor vehicle crashes. From 2000 to 2014, almost 500,000 people lost their lives to drug overdoses.[65] The nondeath implications of the opioid epidemic are also alarming. Nonfatal opioid overdoses can potentially result in anoxic brain injury, nerve palsies, and trauma-related injuries.[66] While the incidences of these complications have not been closely assessed, the high prevalence of opioid-related deaths suggests that such events are not infrequent.

An analysis of the epidemic's evolution over the past 50 years further reveals that 90 percent of people who began using heroin in the past decade were white.[67] Demographically speaking, the health burden of the heroin epidemic has shifted from urban minorities to a wider distribution of people including whites in their late 20s living outside of large urban areas.[68] The potential impact of this health burden on economically depressed, white working-class communities is furthered by declining social capital. Communities buttressed by social support are far less likely to experience the devastation of the opioid epidemic.[69]

Against this backdrop, white working-class families appear to be under considerable duress. To make ends meet, women have increasingly entered the workforce, challenging preexisting notions of white working-class masculinities.[70] Semipermanent domestic arrangements increasingly define the norm. White working-class men in the United States have experienced a decline in their "marriage-market value" through decreased earnings potential, diminished job opportunities, and increased participation in risky or damaging behaviors.[71] The cumulative effect of this domestic demotion is a reduced pool of eligible, "marriageable" men, leading to less marriage overall, lower fertility, and an increase in the proportion of children born to young, unwed mothers in poor, single-parent households.[72] White working-class households also experience high, if not increasing, rates of domestic violence. And the children of these households often face similar violent circumstances once they are on their own.[73]

Just as the future economic fortune of white working-class communities remains to be seen, so does their health forecast. At the height of American industrialization, workers assumed the risks of their jobs with the understanding that unions would fight for their wages and benefits, including health care and workers' compensation.[74] Before and even since the Affordable Care Act (Obamacare), for-profit, employment-based private insurance dominated the American health-care market.[75] Throughout the postwar period, this system largely kept working-class employees, who benefited from long-term union contracts, afloat.[76] With the support of union-arranged health-care benefits, dangerous jobs were, in many respects, normalized as a central feature of the working-class lifestyle.[77] White working-class individuals signed on to a strategic contract with industry: the performance of dangerous work in exchange for a well-earned livelihood. Yet when the jobs left, many workers lost their employer-sponsored health coverage.[78] Interestingly, white working-class individuals have benefited the most from Obamacare.[79] And while the future of the American health-care system remains uncertain, the well-being of white working-class individuals continues to stand in the balance.

### What are the demographics of white working-class people?

These economic, moral, and health narratives obscure an important demographic narrative. Before the Second World War, many industrialized societies were largely racially homogeneous, and mainstream social divisions were grounded in religious or ethnic difference. Indeed, from the founding of the United States through 2004, a majority of Americans were white and had concluded their education without obtaining a four-year university degree.[80] Even as late as the 1990 census, white people without a university degree represented more than 60 percent of American adults—as they do in Britain today. However, with the steady influx of immigrants, weakening fertility rates among the native-born, and an increasingly global economy, the fault lines of sociopolitical relations shifted.[81] As Figures 1.3 and 1.4 show, the last half-century has witnessed the long-term decline of the share of the white population without university degrees in both the United States and the United Kingdom.

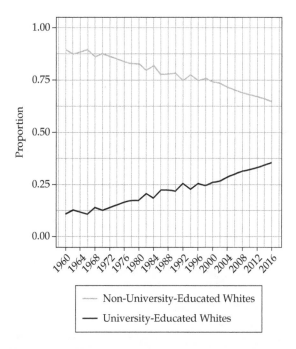

**Figure 1.3** The share of white Americans without university degrees, 1960–2016.
*Source:* American National Election Studies cumulative file.

During this period, immigrants replaced these ethnic whites in lower-skilled positions and in the demographic pipeline. In the United Kingdom, the ethnic minority population has almost doubled since 2004, and minorities account for 80 percent of the country's population growth.[82] The non-white population represented 37 percent of the United States population in 2015, and it is expected to grow, given that the American population under age five is majority non-white.[83] The United States' foreign-born population grew from 9.6 million (4.7 percent) in 1970 to 40 million (12.9 percent) in 2010—the highest share since 1920.[84]

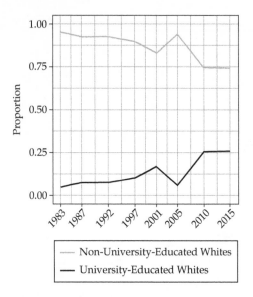

**Figure 1.4** The share of white Britons without university degrees, 1983–2015.
*Source*: British Election Study.

Western democracies have long grappled with how to integrate diverse peoples into economies and societies organized around equal rights. Through all the adjustments, social hierarchies have changed. Whether white people's working-class status is defined based on education, occupation, or income, the white working class in the United States has shrunk by 30 to 50 percent since the Second World War.[85] These trends may be intensified by the extraordinary 22 percent rise in the mortality rate of white working-class people since 1999 while death rates among all other groups have declined.[86]

Still, even with the decline of the British and American manufacturing industries and the countries' ongoing demographic changes, white working-class people represent a significant sector of the voting public. They represent a substantial share of the American and British population as of 2016, depending on how working-class status is understood:

- Sixty-four percent of Britons are white people without a four-year university degree;[87]
- Forty-five percent of Americans are white people without a four-year university degree;[88]
- Fifty-six percent of British families are white households earning less than £60,000 per year;[89] and
- Thirty percent of American families are white households earning less than $60,000 per year.[90]

Unlike Americans, the British working class has shown a propensity to identify as "working class" even when employed in middle-class occupations, some of which require some higher education.

### Where do white working-class people live?

Demographic trends depicting the steadily falling share of white working-class populations are present across a wide range of cities, towns, and countrysides. Figures 1.5 and 1.6 reveal that the loss of white working-class people was especially acute in the American Northeast and West, and in Greater London. Figures 1.7 and 1.8 map the location of the remaining white working-class communities—defined as those that are 85 percent white and under the median national income. In the United States, these counties appear in economically depressed regions, many of which were once central to America's agrarian and manufacturing economies. In Britain, they are dispersed across England, Scotland, and Wales.

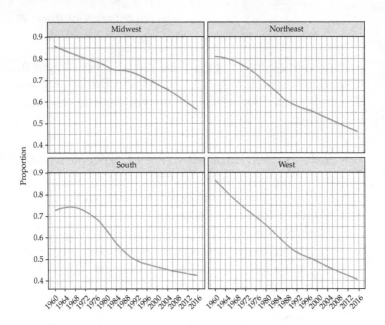

**Figure 1.5** Shares of American population that are white and without a university degree, 1960–2016, by census region.

*Source*: American National Election Studies cumulative file.

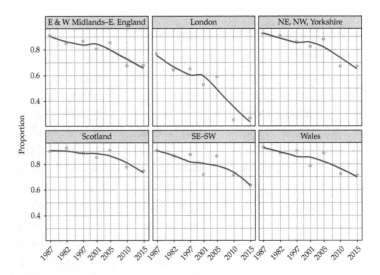

**Figure 1.6** Shares of regional British populations that are white and without a university degree, 1987–2015.

*Source*: British Election Study.

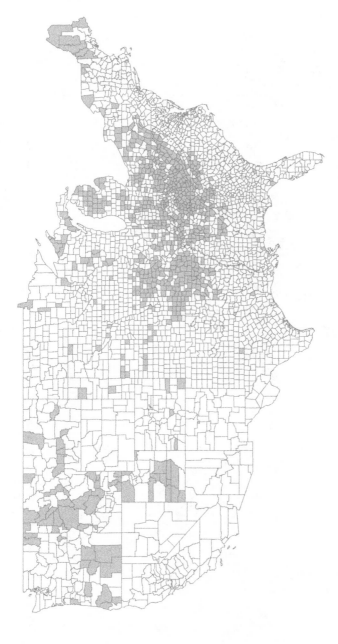

**Figure 1.7** US counties that are 85 percent white or greater and under the national median income highlighted in gray, 2016.

*Source:* 2011–2015 American Community Survey.

**Figure 1.8** UK counties that are 85 percent white or greater and under the national median income highlighted in gray.

*Source:* 2011 UK Census.

However, the narratives of decline are especially pronounced in what I call "post-traumatic" cities. Post-traumatic cities are exurbs and urban communities that lost signature industries in the mid- to late twentieth century and never really recovered. They include Blackburn, Bolton, Hartlepool, Hull, Wolverhampton, and East London in the United Kingdom, and Erie, Flint, Gary, Kenosha, Michigan City, Toledo, and Youngstown in the Rust Belt of the United States, though they also extend throughout the Ohio River Valley, Appalachia, and the Upper Rocky Mountain region. At the peak of North American and European manufacturing economies, particular companies or industries employed enough people for long enough that they could singlehandedly support these cities' economies and dominate their politics. Today, such cities endure as shells of their former splendor.

Two examples of post-traumatic cities are East London in the United Kingdom and Youngstown, Ohio in the United States—where I spent six months conducting fieldwork. East London was planned as a "Garden City," to be anchored by major manufacturers and to lure white working-class East Enders away from London's congested inner city after it became crowded with Eastern European Jewish (and later South Asian) immigrants. In 1922, May & Baker's chemical plant relocated to Dagenham in East London. In 1925, the Barking Power House electric station was established in East London. And in 1931, the Ford Motor Company built what would become an enormous factory on several square miles of Dagenham's riverfront.[91] These employers provided dependable jobs for the residents of the new estate. The population of Dagenham soared from 9,000 to 90,000 between 1921 and 1931, and the combined populations of Barking and Dagenham, then

separate East London boroughs, increased another 50 percent before 1951.

However, after the mid-1970s, East London's economy
went the way of the Ford factory, which endured massive
downsizings. As that industry declined, unions weakened,
markets were deregulated, and industrial jobs followed
a more global move offshore. Britain's postindustrial
economy had little use for East London's white working-
class tradesmen as it shifted to high technology and a
broader service sector.

The area's demographics also altered. A new generation of residents moved in to take advantage of mortgages
and rentals that cost a fraction of those in inner London.
While some purchased homes, many new immigrants
were assigned to public housing in government-owned
rowhouses and tower blocks. As a result, populations
of sub-Saharan Africans, Lithuanians, Bosnians, Poles,
and South Asian Muslims settled across the city. By the
2000s, these immigrant groups composed about half the
population of East London, as an extension of London's
globalizing metropolis.

Youngstown, Ohio, was once known as "Steeltown
USA." Throughout the late 1800s and early 1900s, a thirty-
mile-long stretch of mills developed along the Mahoning
River. For decades, the foundries and furnaces of about
a half-dozen companies provided not only jobs, but also
housing, loans, supporting industries, philanthropy, and
sites for political organization and social life. Rapid population growth fueled the city's rapid industrialization,
thanks to the arrival of working-class immigrants from
every corner of Europe. By 1930, nearly half the city's population owned their homes, and by the 1940s, Youngstown's
population reached 170,000—about 90 percent of which
was white.[92]

These circumstances ended with the swift offshoring of Youngstown's steel industry in the late 1970s and early 1980s. In a matter of six years, Ohio State Employment Services estimates that 50,000 jobs were lost in basic steel and related industries, costing Youngstown's working class $1.3 billion in annual manufacturing wages.[93] Unemployment climbed to a staggering 24.9 percent in 1983 and a wave of personal bankruptcies and foreclosures resulted.[94] The city spiraled into a tailspin characterized by domestic abuse, substance abuse, divorce, suicide, murder, and, ultimately, the mass departure of its population. Today, Youngstown has barely a third of its 1970 population, and about half of its citizens are now black or Latino.

East London and Youngstown are but two examples of cities that have experienced this trauma of simultaneous economic, social, and political collapse. They also represent the more industrialized regions of larger metropolitan areas. There and elsewhere, white working-class people are consumed by a nostalgia that expresses bitter resentment toward the big companies that abandoned their city, a government that did little to stop them from leaving, and a growing share of visible minorities who are altering their neighborhoods' complexion.

Other cities and regions have undergone economic and social decline. However, few places have experienced a decline so universal and so immediate after enjoying the zenith of prosperity. Post-traumatic cities were often so wholly dependent on a single company or sector that their sudden closure or downsizing undercut an entire social, political, and economic infrastructure—depriving their vast communities of the sense of stability, power, and centrality to which they had become accustomed.

The sprawling factories, towering smokestacks, and vast warehouses that once pumped and percolated with the booming business of a past era sit still in the center of cities. Residents maneuver around the crumbling, rusty relics of industrialism in much the same way today's Greeks and Italians maneuver around the roped-off ruins of ancient Athens and Rome. The cities' infrastructure simultaneously taunts inhabitants with memories of better days and also renders false hope that they are one big break from returning to glory.

This pervasive nostalgia depresses innovation and paralyzes the evolution of these communities. And as a result, the characteristic politics of these cities is often backward-facing. Rather than adapt to the post-traumatic future, people seek to reinstate the pre-traumatic past. Small programs have begun to shrink some cities, returning outlying land to nature and clearing the amassed tangle of deserted railroad tracks, electrical lines, and auxiliary piping. But as with urban planning, the politics of modernization are laced with resentment. The chapters that follow break this resentment down into its elemental components.

# 2

# WHITE WORKING-CLASS
# PEOPLE AND IDENTITY

*Is white identity on the rise?*

One of President Trump's most enduring and foreboding achievements may be the reinvigoration of white identity in the United States and beyond. In his social policy proposals and statements during the 2016 American election, he spoke directly to a resentful, anxious constituency of white Americans who felt like they had lost control of their society. He vilified Muslims, cast Mexicans and immigrants as violent opportunists, insulted the disabled, objectified women, undercut American foreign allies, broadbrushed inner cities as war zones, and assailed anyone who shamed his political incorrectness. By the time he praised the "little guy" who was being impoverished and destabilized by a conspiratorial global economy, the race of that "little guy" was quite clear by process of elimination. In championing the views of America's "silent majority," he was addressing white people who have felt as though talking about their identity is off limits.

This direct, deliberate appeal engaged a constituency that had felt forgotten and disrespected by political and business elites for a generation of American politics, but also emboldened them to reassert a more muscular and newly condoned white identity. While news publications would cover a subsequent rise in hate crimes and a renaissance of white supremacy, quietly, white people began to identify more closely with their race. When a nationally representative sample of white Americans was asked "How important is being white to your identity?" the proportion who said "extremely important" nearly doubled from 2012 to 2016 (Figure 2.1).

If a sense of white American solidarity is emerging, it is emerging more among white working-class people. Alongside the earlier question about the importance of being white to one's identity, the survey asked, "How likely is it that many whites are unable to find a job because employers are hiring minorities instead?" and "How important is it that whites work together to change laws that are unfair to whites?" When compared to non-working-class white people, a greater share of white working-class people believed that they were "extremely" likely to lose jobs to minority candidates (Figure 2.2). They were also more likely to believe that it is "extremely" important for white people to work together (Figure 2.3).

These sentiments are increasingly relevant to American politics. New research by Ashley Jardina[1] finds that when white people no longer feel that their power, status, and group privileges are stable and secure, their racial identity becomes salient and politically consequential to their attitudes and decisions. Racial conflict, she argues, is not merely a product of white people's learned out-group racial hostilities or animus; it is also a function of white people's desire to protect their in-group's power and resources.

While British surveys do not measure white identity as thoroughly or to the same extent, the British Social Attitudes Survey offers proxies. In 2013, it asked respondents to what extent they would agree with the following statement: "Britain would begin to lose its

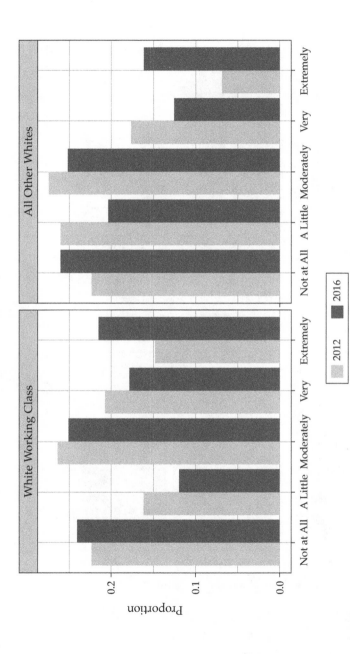

**Figure 2.1** The distribution of white identity among white working-class people and all other whites in 2012 and 2016. "How important is being white to your identity?"

*Source:* 2012 American National Election Studies and 2016 American National Election Studies pilot.

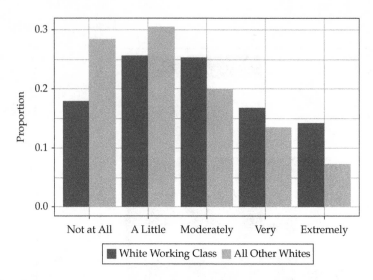

**Figure 2.2** The distribution of responses to "How likely is it that many whites are unable to find a job because employers are hiring minorities instead?"

*Source*: 2016 American National Election Studies pilot.

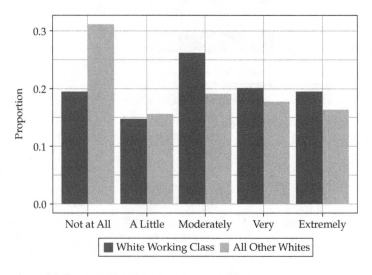

**Figure 2.3** The distribution of responses to "How important is it that whites work together to change laws that are unfair to whites?"

*Source*: 2016 American National Election Studies pilot.

identity if [more people from Eastern Europe (for example, Poland and Latvia)/Muslims/black and (South) Asian people) came to live in Britain." Compared to the bulk of the British population, the response from white working-class people was stunningly nativist—an almost complete inversion of attitudes (Figure 2.4). Respondents were also asked, "Do you think that most white people in Britain would mind or not mind if one of their close relatives were to marry [a person of Asian origin/a person who is Muslim/a person of black African or Caribbean origin]?" Displayed in Figure 2.5, the results again showed that white working-class Britons were less tolerant (or at least would expect less tolerance from their white peers).

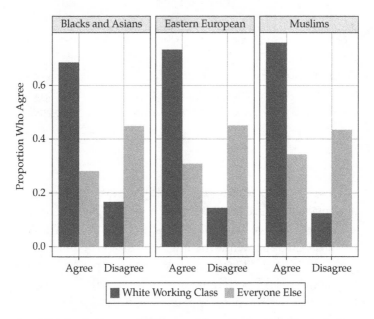

**Figure 2.4** The distribution of responses to "Britain would begin to lose its identity if [more people from Eastern Europe/Muslims/black and Asian people] came to live in Britain"?

*Source*: 2013 British Social Attitudes Survey.

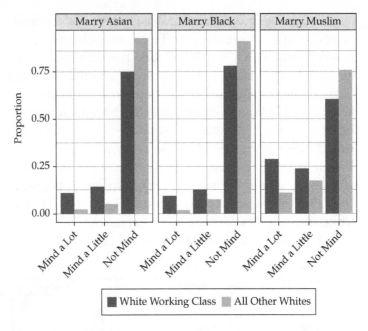

**Figure 2.5** The distribution of responses to "Do you think that most white people in Britain would mind or not mind if one of their close relatives were to marry [a person of Asian origin/a person who is Muslim/a person of black African or Caribbean origin]?"

*Source*: 2013 British Social Attitudes Survey.

Despite this evidence of white identification, belonging, and even solidarity, white working-class people do not appear to believe that their fates are inextricably linked to those of other white people.[2] A survey taken in 2012 and 2016 asked, "Do you think what happens generally to [white/black] people in this country will have something to do with what happens in your life? Will it affect you a lot, some, or not very much?" The responses that white working-class Americans gave showed that they felt their lives were less tied to those of black people and non-working-class white people in 2016 than they were in 2012.[3] Some social scientists believe this concept of "linked fate"—which originated in the study of black Americans—has been improperly extended to other racial and ethnic groups.[4] However, these results may reflect the significant attitudinal differences within the white population—particularly between white people of different social classes, ideologies, and regions. In my previous research, white working-class people expressed a double estrangement, from both racial minorities and white people of higher social standing.

### Why do white working-class people feel marginalized?

For external observers, one of the most perplexing aspects of white working-class politics is white people's sense of marginalization. How can a group with such enduring advantages and power lament their weakness? The answer lies in relativity.

To the external observer, the structural advantages for white people in North America and Europe are quite plain. White people benefit from a political and social system of their own creation. They are advantaged by a history of discrimination in their favor, a trajectory unfettered by the legacies of slavery or the exploitation of colonialism. They boast an acquaintance with norms of national culture and language. White males in particular assume the "privileged role of universal subject."[5] They enjoy an intangible affinity with predominantly white leaders in business and politics, and they need not worry about adapting their behavior or expectations to this environment. Some describe the situation in harsher terms: White people exploit "unearned advantages" as a means to "improve or maintain their social position."[6] Earned or unearned, it is assumed that these advantages make white individuals the incumbents.

However, white working-class people are consumed by a sense of loss. While they acknowledge histories of advantage and the oppression of minorities, many neither recognize the endurance of these advantages nor believe that their working-class families had a hand in the oppression of yesteryear. Rather, many believe that their societies and governments have compensated for sins of the past by subordinating white working-class people today—scapegoating them and crafting a global system that leads to their poverty, disempowerment, and, ultimately, their extinction. Accordingly, they view attempts to "level the playing field" as the relative loss of the status they once held or as unnecessary after the recalibrations of the Civil Rights Era. Since the end of the Manufacturing Era and the coinciding Civil Rights Movement, white working-class people have experienced three principal changes—the incorporation of immigrants who compete for work and resources, the loss of political power, and the emergence of social norms that value diversity and discount heritage. Accordingly, there are three components to their marginality.

*Outnumbering:* White working-class people recognize the steady deterioration of their numbers. Increasing proportions of all population groups are attaining higher levels of education and white people comprise a decreasing share of national populations in the United States and the United Kingdom.[7] By 2044, the US Census estimates that white people generally will make up less than 50 percent of the American population. However, this change will be even more pronounced on the local level as the share of white working-class people in neighborhoods and cities falls. Such change is attributable to fertility rates, foreigners moving in, and whites moving out.

In the United States, 20 percent of counties experienced a 10 percent or greater decrease in their white population between 1991 and 2011. About 5 percent of American counties went from being majority white in 1991 to minority white in 2011. In the United Kingdom, 15.5 percent of local authorities experienced a 10 percent or greater decrease in their white population between 1991 and 2001—a shorter period than what was measured in the United States. About 5 percent of British local authorities went from being majority white in 1991 to minority white in 2001.

In my interview with a white community activist in East London, she would stop me if I referred to immigrant-origin groups as "minorities." "It's a fact that we are a minority," she asserted. "There's not a school in the borough that's not eighty percent ethnic. Nobody English moves into this borough. They only move out. It's gotten to the stage where, even queuing for the loo, it's a novelty when you meet an English person to speak to. . . . I won't allow myself to feel on the outside of my society. But a lot of other people are scared. They feel intimidated." Nancy's statements reflect a generally monolithic view of non-white, non-English people that is shared by many in her neighborhood.

*Exclusion:* White working-class people express a sense that they lack representation not just in government, but also in popular culture, public institutions, and employment. They are wary that the same principles of equal access and representation that compensate for other groups' disadvantages do not apply to them. Only 2 percent of those currently serving in Congress can claim working-class backgrounds.[8] The *Washington Post* reports that between 1984 and 2009, the median net worth of a member of the House of Representatives grew from

$280,000 to $725,000 in inflation-adjusted dollars, while the wealth of an American family slightly declined from $20,600 to $20,500.[9] As a result, government and business feel distant, clubby, and unwelcoming.

In Youngstown, Ohio, a 29-year-old chef told me that his disempowerment extends to the workplace. "Whites are the minority now," he said. "Sometimes, it gives [black people] greater power because it's the higher group. So they can get their way. My uncle works at a plant where everybody is scared to tell the black people what to do because they're worried about retaliation. The managers are outnumbered and they don't have a backbone. . . . White people are held to a different standard. In history books, whites were always above the blacks. But we desegregated to change the world. It's been one hundred years and they still want more." Paradoxically, he implied that black people are privileged in the United States, while simultaneously acknowledging that white people continue to occupy most positions of authority.

In surveys, white working-class people are more likely to deny the advantages that white people continue to possess, and they express a sense that they are subject to unique disadvantages that reinforce their exclusion from mainstream society. A nationally representative sample of Americans was asked, "Does being white help you, hurt you, or make no difference for you personally in today's society?" A near majority of white working-class people believed that being white made no difference to their fate (Figure 2.6). Meanwhile, white working-class people in the same sample were more likely than other demographics to believe their whiteness hurt them. In another metric, the sample of people were asked, "How many disadvantages do white people have that minorities do not have in today's society?" (See Figure 2.7.) Compared to the rest of those surveyed, white working-class people were far less likely to say "none."

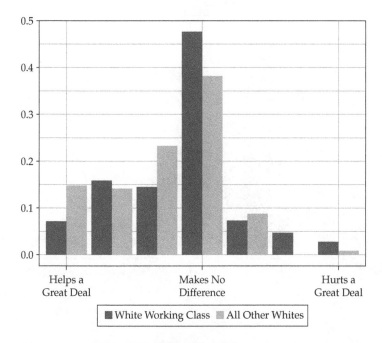

**Figure 2.6** Distribution of responses to "Does being white help you, hurt you, or make no difference for you personally in today's society?" among the white working class and everyone else.

*Source:* 2016 American National Election Studies pilot.

*Discrimination:* Many white working-class people believe they are frequently subject to conscious or unconscious prejudgment by members of ethnic minorities and middle- and upper-class white people. They believe that such prejudice affects their ability to get jobs, receive equal treatment by officials and businesses, and access government benefits like housing or welfare. Sometimes, this is also a matter of the special treatment white working-class people believe members of non-white minorities receive—such as scholarships, employment, exemptions or leniencies, and government contracting. "I fought for this country," lamented a pensioner I interviewed in

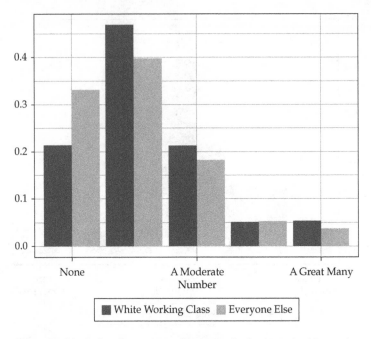

**Figure 2.7** Distribution of responses to "How many disadvantages do white people have that minorities do not have in today's society?" among the white working class and everyone else.

*Source*: 2016 American National Election Studies pilot.

East London, "and it ain't even our country anymore. You're not the priority. We've got everything here. Gays, lesbians—what do you call them?—bisexuals, prostitutes, pedophiles. This place is like [the soap operas] 'Coronation Street' meets 'East Enders' and 'Holly Oaks' all at once." In Youngstown, an electrician told me, "White people have become the minority itself. . . . People have freaked out on me for things I've said, because I can't say anything [about black people] because of slavery and their historical oppression. [Black] people aren't looking for equality; they're looking for retaliation." While the pensioner refers to her loss of priority beneath people she finds deviant, the electrician does not mind relegation so long as it promotes actual equality. However, many white working-class individuals view the struggle for equal treatment as a vengeful persecution—a campaign to demote white people, rather than to promote others.

In surveys, white working-class people reveal a greater sensitivity to discrimination in all forms—as it hinders their own pursuits, but also as it hinders other constituencies. The same, nationally representative survey asked whether its American respondents agree that there is "a great deal" or "a lot of" discrimination against various groups in the United States, including blacks, Christians, Hispanics, Muslims, whites, women, and gays, lesbians, bisexuals, and transgender people (Figure 2.8). White working-class

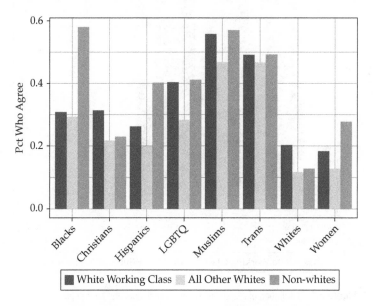

**Figure 2.8** Proportion of white working-class, white non-working-class, and non-white respondents who agree that there is a great deal or a lot of discrimination against each group in the United States.

*Source*: 2016 American National Election Studies pilot.

people were more likely than non-working-class whites to acknowledge prejudice against all the named groups. However, white working-class people perceived discrimination against blacks, Hispanics, and women far less than non-whites, and they perceived discrimination against whites and Christians more than all others. In another metric, the sample was asked, "In general, does the federal government treat whites better than blacks, treat blacks better than whites, or treat them both about the same?" (Figure 2.9). White working-class people were more likely to believe the government reserved "much better" treatment for black people.

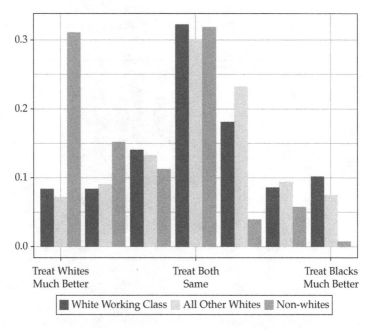

**Figure 2.9** Distribution of responses to "In general, does the federal government treat whites better than blacks, treat blacks better than whites, or treat them both about the same?" among white working-class, non-working-class white, and non-white respondents.

*Source*: 2016 American National Election Studies pilot.

## Is it reasonable to think of white working-class people as a "minority"?

While I was conducting research in white working-class communities, no small number of people reported feeling like a "minority." Classifying any group of American or British white people as a minority is dubious at best. Such a relabeling contradicts 50 years of social programs, civil-rights struggles, and government policies that refer to people of color as "minorities." At their inception, such efforts acknowledged—and indeed were mobilized against—the privileged status and greater numerical power of white people.

The plight of white working-class people challenges conventional considerations of what a "minority" is. Minority status has typically been equated with smaller numbers and persistent legacies of disadvantage.[10] In particular, social scientists have defined a minority as "a group of people who, because of their physical or cultural characteristics, are singled out from the others in the society in which they live for differential and unequal treatment, and who therefore regard themselves as objects of collective discrimination."[11] This definition bars any claim of minority status by white people, whose physical characteristics have allowed them to evade such discrimination and instead employ it to their advantage. However, do poor white people share the same advantages enjoyed by wealthy white people?

White working-class people lead us to question whether being a minority is—alongside socioeconomic disadvantage, histories of disempowerment, discrimination, and demography—fundamentally a matter of race. If the concept of a "minority" cannot apply to white people, its utility may be limited. How useful is a concept that cannot be applied across populations? Alternatively, if minority status is not necessarily a matter of race, we need to consider that minority status plausibly could be claimed by groups that experience similar levels and types of disempowerment similar (if not comparable) to people of color.

The objective study of white working-class people also demands that we consider their claims of disadvantage. Researchers, like me, who study ethnic minorities generally view these diverse groups sympathetically in light of their structural disadvantages, whether economic, educational, or cultural. The challenge is to sustain this empathy for those who stand as the primary antagonists to ethnic minorities. White working-class people complicate understandings of marginality because the system they are challenging is one that has empowered them for centuries.

*Socioeconomic Disempowerment:* Political systems have institutionalized inequality for both poor white and nonwhite people in the United States and United Kingdom. These democracies are predominantly "elite-led" and concerned with the preferences of higher-income voters.[12] Yet even if governments were more accountable to common citizens, researchers have identified tendencies that reinforce inequality. In the United States, as income inequality grows, support for redistribution of wealth shrinks.[13] Surprisingly, this relationship holds for individuals in both the top and the bottom quintiles of income.

When they do have a say about economic assistance from the government, white working-class communities are prone to "welfare chauvinism," where xenophobia and racism distract from policies that would otherwise benefit them. More ethnically diverse societies display less support for redistribution, often because voters believe that the recipients are undeserving.[14] Voters tend to vote against their economic interests to support social or culturally aligned agendas. Particularly in the American South, cultural considerations can be so important that income and voter choice have no correlation.[15]

Furthermore, segregation by income and education is accelerating beyond any historical precedent in America. As a result of modern transportation, social insurance programs, and a more efficient "college sorting machine," Americans are now sorting themselves geographically along class lines.[16] Over time, this self-segregation results in less social mobility.

*Psychological Disempowerment:* Given growing inequality, recent scholarship in psychology also demonstrates a set of contradictory tendencies among people that reinforce their immobility. A sociological and psychological literature on "system justification theory" traces people's tendency to support and justify the status quo, particularly inequality and social hierarchies, as fair and legitimate.[17] Driven by their desire to reduce uncertainty in their lives, people tend to engage in system justification by forming stereotypes that rationalize status differences between groups—commonly by attributing more moral worth to the advantaged than to the disadvantaged.[18]

However, even if white working-class constituencies were to develop a sense of collective grievance and a desire to organize, they lack an identity around which they may mobilize. Poorer white people and poorer ethnic minorities are subject to the same class position, but it is less often recognized that similar structural inequalities trap all economically disadvantaged people. These organizational difficulties affect how white working-class people make political claims and define themselves.[19]

And unlike poor minorities, poor whites tend to lack the social bonds that can help reduce marginality.[20] Social scientists have found that black working-class individuals exhibit more collectivism than their white counterparts, a unity formed around black "cultural resources," such as the shared experience of fighting together against racial segregation and discrimination.[21] White workers do not have access to these same cultural resources and subsequently tend to be more individualistic.

Such perceptions also connect with psychological research on individuals' "locus of control" or their understanding of the extent to which they can control events that affect their life.[22] A sense of powerlessness may encourage the working class to withdraw from politics, which then further diminishes their influence. Table 2.1 summarizes different groups' perceptions of their political power, based on original, nationally representative surveys of Britons and Americans. We see that perceptions of political power are weakest among those without university educations, those who identify as working class, and those who are middle-aged.

White working-class communities' tendency to self-segregate or justify their disadvantage is reinforced—or perhaps inspired—by the way society regards them. Over time, the most disadvantaged "white people" have been made to feel like outsiders by terms such as "white trash," "redneck," and "chav."[23] Such words stigmatize the white working class, and the stereotypes that accompany them reduce their opportunities for success. There is a tendency for people to fulfill the stereotypes that others apply to them—in a much more pronounced way than they otherwise would if the stereotype did not exist.[24] And while stigma against white working-class people may be less intense than others applied to ethnic minorities, it is more socially accepted in light of the other advantages white people enjoy.

*Political Disempowerment*: Compounding systemic and psychological factors, political factors exert more downward pressure. American leaders and government are less likely to direct their communications to marginalized communities, who may be less likely to vote.[25] People with low political awareness are consequently less likely

|  | United Kingdom Mean | United States Mean |
|---|---|---|
| *Education* | | |
| University Education | 3.88 | 4.46 |
| No University Education | 3.53 | 3.38 |
| *Age* | | |
| 18–24 | 3.99 | 3.97 |
| 25–39 | 3.78 | 4.27 |
| 40–59 | 3.54 | 3.31 |
| 60+ | 3.73 | 3.47 |
| *Self-Reported Social Class* | | |
| Upper | 4.02 | 6.07 |
| Middle | 3.71 | 4.28 |
| Lower Middle | 3.54 | N/A* |
| White Working | 3.25 | 2.81 |
| *Gender* | | |
| Male | 3.79 | 3.86 |
| Female | 3.60 | 3.58 |

**Table 2.1** Perceptions of Personal Power:
The extent to which British respondents agree that "people like me have political power" on a scale from 0 to 10. A 10 indicates that the respondent thinks that "people like me have a lot of political power" and a 0 indicates that "people like me don't have any political power." White working class here is defined as white and having no university education.

*In the United Kingdom, class is measured using the British National Readership Survey social grade scale. There is no equivalent in US surveys.

to change their attitudes about political issues. As a result, political parties tend to divert their efforts and resources to citizens with higher levels of reception to their outreach, typically those in the middle classes and above—creating a self-reinforcing loop. The result is that marginalized communities are ignored. In a British study, many poor white voters experienced more face-to-face contact with extremist party campaigners than campaigners from mainstream parties, who lack an active and visible presence in poor white communities.[26]

Until only recently, the two-party systems in the United States and Britain have not offered white working-class people a clear political outlet for over a generation. During 13 years of a Labour government, from 1996 to 2010, and 16 years of recent Democratic presidential administrations, little attention was paid to the specific interests of the white working class—the parties' one-time bases. For the Left, a principal turning point was the decline of the Manufacturing Era, the collapse of union strength, and the coincidental rise of the Civil Rights Movement. In the aftermath, left-wing parties increasingly aligned with a cosmopolitan financial class, ethnic minorities, and urban liberals. In the United States' realignment, the Republicans subsequently pursued white working-class people's votes with appeals to social causes. However, the Conservative Party's reluctance to do so (and their historical association with the aristocracy) in Britain left white working-class people to unenthusiastically settle on Labour or to back fringe parties like the British National Party or UKIP.[27] Table 2.2 summarizes different groups' perceptions of politicians' care for their interests. From the same surveys, we see that perceptions of politicians' interest in them are lowest amongst working class people, those without university educations, and those who are middle-aged or older.

In the past 10 years, we have witnessed the rising salience and support of Radical Right and populist political parties in Europe and right-wing movements in the United States. In particular, the growth in the population of ethnic minorities in Western European countries has, in several countries, driven increased support for the extreme Right.[28] Despite this support, the success of Radical Right parties across countries is largely determined by differences in

|  | United Kingdom Mean | United States Mean |
|---|---|---|
| *Education* | | |
| University Education | 3.93 | 4.38 |
| No University Education | 3.49 | 3.46 |
| *Age* | | |
| 18–24 | 4.11 | 3.99 |
| 25–39 | 3.66 | 4.38 |
| 40–59 | 3.42 | 3.47 |
| 60+ | 3.93 | 3.24 |
| *Self-Reported Social Class* | | |
| Upper | 4.12 | 5.32 |
| Middle | 3.75 | 4.08 |
| Lower Middle | 3.47 | N/A* |
| White Working | 3.14 | 2.94 |
| *Gender* | | |
| Male | 3.64 | 3.89 |
| Female | 3.74 | 3.61 |

**Table 2.2** Perceptions of Politicians' Care:
Distribution of responses to what extent "politicians care a lot about people like me" on a scale from 0 to 10. A 10 indicates that the respondent thinks that "people like me have a lot of political power" and a 0 indicates that "politicians don't care about people like me." White working class here is defined as white and having no university education.

*In the United Kingdom, class is measured using the British National Readership Survey social grade scale. There is no equivalent in US surveys.

electoral systems.[29] Proportional representation and coalition governments reduce strategic voting among Radical Right supporters, who may feel incentivized to back a fringe candidate.[30] However, in first-past-the-post electoral systems like those of the United States and the United Kingdom, the relative difficulty of supporting such parties and movements (and their subsequent lack of success) has led significant numbers of individuals to disengage from the political process—until they were energized by the Trump and Brexit campaigns.

### Why is immigration so pivotal to white working-class politics?

In light of the party coalitions established after the American political realignment in the 1960s and cemented during the Obama presidency, cross-party "vote switching" is exceedingly rare in the United States. However, a significant number of people who voted for Democrats in 2012 (or did not vote at all) cast votes for Donald Trump in 2016. The political scientists Loren Collingwood, Tyler Reny, and Ali Valenzuela have found that the principal driver for this switch is a backlash against immigration among white working-class people. Inversely, individuals with positive views about immigration were most likely to switch from the Republican Party to vote for Hillary Clinton.[31] Similarly, during the Brexit campaign, no policy issue was more salient than immigration. These debates were not so much about Left versus Right or liberal versus conservative, as in previous cycles. Rather, the elections turned on the debate over open versus closed, globalism versus nationalism.

In such an environment, immigration offers the whole polemical package. It features the politics of job creation. Do immigrants create new jobs with all the businesses they start and products they innovate? Do they accept and perform unwanted jobs? Or do they compete with natives for jobs? It features the politics of trade. Do immigrants undermine unions or bolster them? Do immigrants keep companies from offshoring work? Do companies exploit temporary labor visas to replace the native-born? It features the politics of welfare. Are immigrants net recipients of or net contributors to the welfare state? It features the politics of criminal justice. Is immigration enforcement deporting valuable contributors to society and destroying families? Are we letting criminals stay? It features the politics of foreign affairs. Do countries have a humanitarian obligation to welcome refugees? Are immigrants a source of international terrorism?

Most of all, immigration features the politics of identity. The fire of nationalism is stoked by immigration because the arrival of newcomers raises broad, existential questions about how a nation should be defined and what its future ought to be. Based on what criteria should we select immigrants? What predicts or prepares people for integration? According to what standards should we integrate newcomers? What are the qualifications for being an American? What are British values? There are no easy answers to such questions, particularly when these countries are already quite diverse, and narrow understandings would alienate large numbers of citizens. Modernity has seen the questioning, reinterpretation, and evolution of orthodoxies in every regard. This has revived efforts to reinforce (and re-create) national understandings of heritage, but it also has fostered a recognition that there is strength in diversity.

The native-born—not merely white people—always understand their national identity with more complexity and nuance than they understand the identity of newcomers. Consequently, immigrants' culture and attributes always appear far more strident and unified than one's own. This truth was inadvertently expressed by *Financial Times* columnist Christopher Caldwell in his alarmist book about the threat Muslims pose to European democracies, *Reflections on the Revolution in Europe*. In it, he referred to European societies as "hospitable," "insecure," and "malleable." In contrast, he depicted Islam as "anchored," "confident," and "adversarial." However, Islam is a religion with dozens of sects, thousands of traditions, and a cacophony of beliefs that has left it irreconcilably splintered. Imagine how "anchored," "confident," and "adversarial" European states appear when they are able to align into a 27-country supranational union.

Of course, those inside the European Union perceive a thin consensus and threats to national sovereignty. For many white working-class people there, the EU and its open internal borders represent precisely the threat that globalization poses. Many Americans are similarly perturbed by how the movement of people, money, and culture blurs national distinctions—cheapening them by endowing newcomers with membership, bending to accommodate their differences, and importing commercial and cultural products from overseas. This is a far greater threat both to people who do not have the resources to make use of these products and opportunities and to people who derive their self-worth from their sense of heritage.

According to the survey data presented in Figures 2.10 and 2.11, white working-class people place greater value in heritage-based attributes than all others when defining the American and British identities. More than the general American population, white people without university degrees believe that, to be truly American, people need to have American ancestry, American traditions, an American birth, and fluency in English. More than the general British population, white working-class respondents believed that, to be truly British, people needed to have British ancestry, a British birth, and, in some cases, Christian faith. These factors don't accord with official qualifications for American and British citizenship. While immigrant admissions were once explicitly or implicitly dictated by race and ethnic heritage, requirements since the 1960s have focused on length of residency and good conduct. As the ranks of American and British citizens swell with people from Africa, Asia,

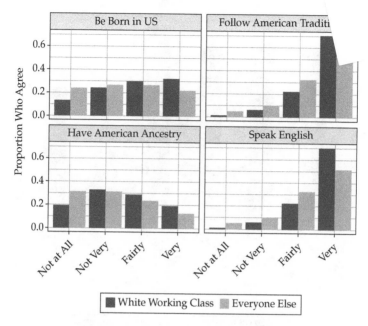

**Figure 2.10** The distribution of responses to "To be truly American, how important is it to . . . ?" among the white working class and everyone else.

*Source:* 2016 American National Election Studies.

Latin America, and the Middle East, heritage is perceived to be devalued.

Ultimately, any country that offers the possibility of naturalization must recognize that the composition of their society will change with immigration—that there is no such thing as "full assimilation." However, this truth has been hard to accept for many in Europe, where national identities can theoretically be traced back to antiquity. It has also been controversial in settler states like the United States. In a precursor to Caldwell's Muslim panic, the political scientist Samuel Huntington published a book that similarly warned of the threat posed by Latin Americans— Mexicans in particular. Huntington argued that the

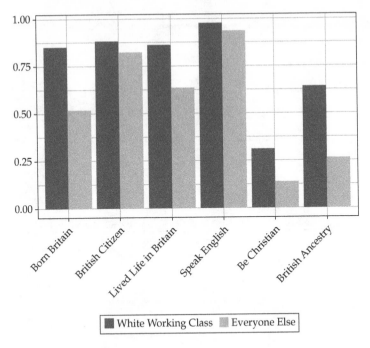

**Figure 2.11** The distribution of responses to "Some people say that the following things are important for being truly British. Others say they are not important. How important do you think each of the following is?" among the white working class and everyone else.

*Source*: 2013 British Social Attitudes Survey.

United States was defined by an "Anglo-Protestant creed" throughout its history, and that all immigrants assimilated into this creed until it fell "under assault by diversity." Mexicans, he argued, had the capacity to alter that creed because of their size, concentration, proximity, and refusal to integrate.

Subsequent research has demonstrated that Mexicans and other Latinos integrate into the United States very well, particularly considering that most arrive with fewer resources than other immigrants.[32] Yet Huntington's book was an example of the type of concerns raised by demographic change. It was very aptly titled: *Who Are We?*

### Is white working-class angst merely racism?

Racism is a powerful word. It's the right way to describe the long history of prejudice and discrimination against people on the basis of their looks and ancestry. It's also important to identify, in modern society, the link between contemporary expressions of racism and earlier injustices, such as the enslavement of blacks or the genocide of native people. While they may not be equivalent, employer discrimination against Muslims, police profiling of Latinos, housing discrimination against blacks—enduring forms of racism—are thus rightly seen as legacies of past oppression. This is valuable because it contextualizes the choices and policies of contemporary societies in a troubled history of race.

However, many white working-class people see current claims of racism as a means by which to unfairly disqualify their viewpoints by linking them to their ancestors' past misdeeds. In the view of many disaffected white working-class people, it's crucial to talk frankly, even critically, about the perils of Islam, immigration, and the Black Lives Matter movement, even if it means offending some listeners. Some of these voters see suppression of their ideas as part of a broader conspiracy to impose a globalist worldview. This perception was seized by leaders like Donald Trump in the United States and Nigel Farage, who led UKIP and the Brexit Leave campaign. The two men elevated hearsay to podiums and shouted the very ideas that supporters have been too intimidated to mutter under their breaths. "We cannot afford to be so politically correct anymore," Trump said in his July 2016 Republican National Convention speech.

While many views held by white working-class people scapegoat minority groups for broader social problems—often based on stereotypes, myths, and prejudice—it is important to acknowledge that even well-meaning conservative critiques of social policies have been tarnished by far less valid accusations of racism. A key problem is that racism imposes a binary on any statement, action, or person: He or she is either racist, or not. Yet many viewpoints occupy the space in between—perhaps informed by racial resentment, or perhaps absent of racial animus but regarding a racially charged issue, but not supremacist. Is it racist to be averse to immigration because it is part of the global system of commerce displacing and destabilizing work? Is it racist to lament the poor state of white working-class representation at the highest levels of governance? Is it racist to advocate against affirmative action policies on principles of equal consideration? The answers to these questions are subjective.

During my fieldwork in the United Kingdom and the United States, dozens of my respondents would preface their most candid thoughts to me by stating "I'm not a racist, but . . ." Sometimes, what followed was unequivocally racist; but in many other cases, their subsequent statements had little to do with race. Why then was this preface so widely used?

Rather, they were concerned that their ideas would be disqualified, when they were, in fact, sincere expressions about how their societies are being transformed. For many white working-class people, racism is perceived to be a "mute button." We have all heard or witnessed people's views rhetorically invalidated or disqualified on the grounds that they are racist—by both white people and minorities. White working-class people feel doubly estranged. They feel estranged from minority groups, who they believe have access to new privileges that compensate for historic advantages that today's white working-class people do not recall exploiting. And they feel alienated from an urban white bourgeoisie that has divorced their less skilled or geographically isolated co-ethnics and look down upon them. Further, they feel blamed for neither empathizing with the plight of minorities nor pulling themselves out of poverty and embracing global cosmopolitanism. Therefore, the preface "I'm not racist" is not a disclaimer, but rather an exhortation to listen and not dismiss or invalidate the claims of a group that feels marginalized.

Interestingly, those respondents who were able to more specifically articulate their frustration often framed it in the civil rights themes of equality and justice. An unemployed 18-year-old Londoner said, "You go for an interview and most of the employers are Asians. Basically, they're discriminating against us, and we were here first. I have some training as a retail sales assistant. But when I've submitted my CV, I've been told that I can't apply because I'm not Asian. . . . I feel like I'm beneath them." The vast majority of my subjects did not belong to white supremacist groups. Many white working-class individuals simply view the broader struggle against racism as one that demotes white people, rather than promotes others to equal ground.

The specter of racism is inevitable in such discussions. However, as societies struggle to level the proverbial playing field, rather than view this process as the elevation of ethnic minorities to equality, many white working-class people only perceive their relative loss of status. They are consumed by a sense of relegation. The data presented thus far depict a constituency of white working-class people that, with the decline of unions, industry, and social status, are more attached to their amorphous racial identity and national heritage, and more sensitive to people's prejudice against them. They are also less inclined to recognize the legacies of disadvantage that endure for ethnic minorities today precisely because it discounts the struggles of white working-class people. Indeed, their legacies of advantage are for white working-class people what the ocean is for fish: When you've been swimming in it all your life, you don't even know it's there.

# 3

# WHITE WORKING-CLASS ATTITUDES AND BELIEFS

*What are white working-class partisan trends?*

United States

One of the most staggering trends in American politics is the utter collapse of white working-class support for the Democratic Party over the last 50 years. The trend is as extraordinary for its steadiness as it is for its duration. Figure 3.1 displays this remarkable realignment in the demographics of the American Left since the Civil Rights Movement in the 1960s. After peaking at 61 percent in 1964, white working-class support for the Democratic Party fell to a mere 35 percent in 2016. Over this period, the trend has not been limited to a particular region of the United States. Figure 3.2 shows that the collapse was universal but particularly pronounced in the American South and West. The numbers stand in sharp contrast to partisan trends among the remainder of the American population, which has reported greater Democratic appeal outside of the South over the same period. The downward slope was also not interrupted by the victories of Democratic presidents Bill Clinton and Barack Obama. White working-class Democratic identification dropped by 10 points nationwide after Barack Obama was elected in 2008. It is worth emphasizing that this all preceded Donald Trump's ascent.

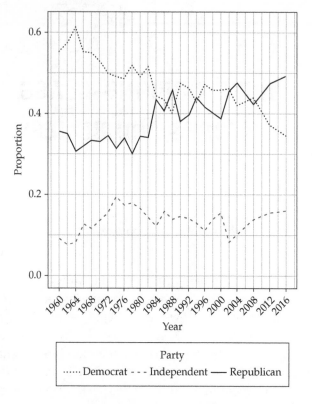

**Figure 3.1** Self-reported party identification among white working-class Americans, 1960–2016. Weak partisans and leaners were combined with strong partisans.
*Source*: American National Election Studies cumulative file.

Contrary to popular perception, President Trump did not cultivate frustration among white working-class people; he harvested it.

Who are the white working-class people who have most recently stopped identifying with the Democratic Party and embraced Donald Trump? In my fieldwork, I distinguished between two types of people. First, there are those who support Trump primarily because they agree with the authoritarian, nationalist moral order he sought

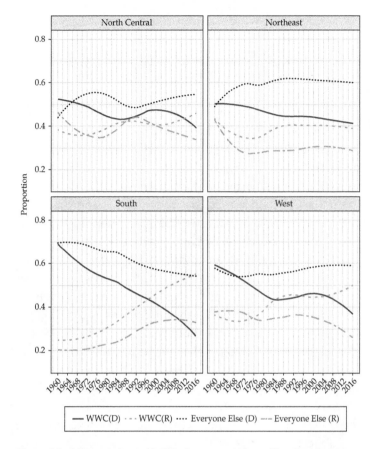

**Figure 3.2** Self-reported party identification among white working-class Americans and all others by region, 1960–2016. Weak partisans and leaners were combined with strong partisans.

*Source*: American National Election Studies cumulative file.

to establish. I call them the Nationalists. Second, there are those who support Trump primarily because they believed he embodied a cleansing of establishment politics that has left white working-class people poorer and forgotten over recent decades. I call them the Exasperated. The Democrats might never hope to gain the support of

Nationalists, for whom Trump is a messianic figure—but they might hope to gain the support of the Exasperated, who are wary of Trump and voted for him out of frustration with the past few decades of politics, embodied by Hillary Clinton.

The Nationalists represent an enduring cult of personality. They will be pleased by Trump's executive orders limiting immigration and punishing sanctuary cities, not even necessarily because they disdain immigrants, but rather because of what immigrants represent. When I spoke to them, these voters sensed that they were losing control of their country and its identity, that they were losing their place in the social hierarchy. Trump's "America First" approach comforts them and reinforces the supremacy of white people. Trump is likely to maintain Nationalist support until the bitter end, even if he is unable to deliver the economic prosperity he promised, and even if his social agenda is ruled unconstitutional. He will inevitably blame others, and this constituency will buy into what he says. Short of a microphone capturing him trashing these supporters behind their backs, they represent his die-hard base. Nationalists likely left the Democratic Party before the 1990s and are unlikely to return. They occupy the Republican Party's far-right flank.

The Exasperated are different. They have likely voted for Democrats and Republicans over the years, seeking someone who would champion their economic and emotional cause. They feel betrayed by the countless politicians who have stood in front of still-shuttered mills and smelters and promised to bring manufacturing and mining economies back to life. It's why they have swung from party to party, from year to year—often reacting to the failures of previous candidates to deliver. It's why so many of them voted for Obama after previously voting for George W. Bush, and Bill Clinton before that. In Figure 3.1, we can see a steady rise in the number of white working-class people who identify as Independent since 2000. This is present across all regions of the United States, but it is more poignant in post-traumatic cities and regions that feature people with protectionist economic attitudes that supersede any social conservatism. They are not "Independent" so much as constantly disappointed.

Their disappointment stems from their dismissal by both Democrats and Republicans since the end of the Manufacturing Era. Since that period, Republicans have been unsure how to appeal to the Exasperated without compromising the party's ties to business. The Exasperated also harbor significant distrust for establishment Republicans, as British working class voters have for Conservatives. For their part, Democrats seem to view the Exasperated as an enigmatic, troublesome family member—one that they see in November every two years for obligatory reasons but from which they otherwise would prefer to maintain a safe distance. They are confused about how to mobilize greater turnout among people who are so distrustful of the government and harbor more culturally conservative views than much of the Democratic coalition.

This has not been a bitter struggle for appeal between Right and Left. Rather, both sides have determined that wooing the Exasperated risks complicating their established coalitions. While the Left would benefit the most from the unification of the (white and non-white) working class in the short term, they are reluctant to risk their relationship with more socially liberal and diverse voting blocs who have invigorated their coalition. More implicitly, they may also be wary of turning off elite moderates who fear the inflammation of class divisions. For now, both establishments are reluctant to invest in the Exasperated as a constituency. They are viewed as untouchable.

The candidacy of Donald Trump posed a direct challenge to this logic. While party elites avoided a direct appeal to the Exasperated out of electoral concerns, Trump has tapped into this neglected set of voters by crafting himself as an Independent infiltrating the party system. The Exasperated voted against Clinton in 2016 because, as a longtime member of the Washington establishment, she portended more broken promises. They voted for Trump because he was the first politician in a generation to make a deliberate pitch for their support. Many of the Exasperated remain wary of President Trump. He filled his administration and Cabinet with business elites who profited from the foreclosure of American homes and the offshoring of American businesses. And they are savvy enough to distinguish between the salvation of a single factory and the salvation of an industry. They are more likely to recognize when Trump presses for tax cuts for the wealthy before raising the federal minimum wage, when Trump takes away Obamacare without replacing it with something better, or when Trump fails to deliver on the jobs he promised. They have adopted a "wait and see" approach.

## United Kingdom

Trends in the United Kingdom reveal a more universal sense of exasperation among white working-class people. Figure 3.3 shows how they were enthralled by the firm nationalism of Margaret Thatcher in the 1980s, and were offered hope by Tony Blair's New Labour in the 1990s. However, as neoliberalism left white working-class people no better off and ultimately excluded from the global economy, there began a decline in Labour support. Unlike previous eras, when the Conservative Party could profit, white working-class people have been hesitant to back David Cameron and subsequently Theresa May, leading to two hung Parliaments

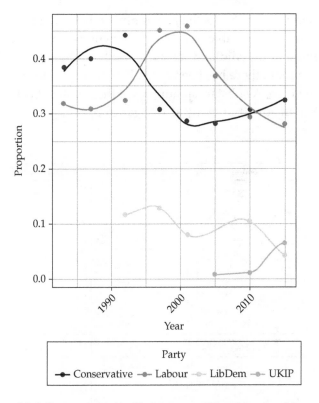

**Figure 3.3** Self-reported party identification among white working-class Britons, 1983–2015.

*Source*: British Election Study.

during their tenures. During this period of disenchantment, no party emerged to represent white working-class people until the United Kingdom Independence Party (UKIP) in the 2015 general election. The rise of UKIP accounts for many lost Labour votes and the Conservatives' inability to take advantage. With UKIP's hiatus (due to disorderly infighting and the absence of Parliamentary seats) in the aftermath of the Brexit referendum, white working-class people were left with three parties, each of which appears out of touch with their interests.

Figure 3.4 exhibits the geography of these trends. While the Tories were able to pick up new voters from Labour's demise in the Midlands and the South of England outside of London, there has been a steady or steep fall for Labour elsewhere. A substantial number of these voters flocked to UKIP in 2015, but many also began supporting nationalist

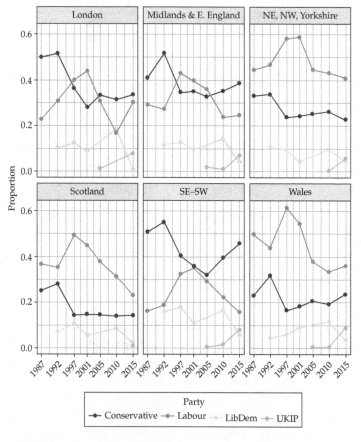

**Figure 3.4** Self-reported party identification among white working-class Britons by region, 1987–2015.

*Source*: British Election Study.

parties in Scotland, Wales, and Northern Ireland (not shown in the figures). Many have also sat out. Labour's support has been decimated, and they have had no relief from previously reliable Labour districts in the North of England—where many white working-class people live in postindustrial towns and cities. This picture reveals significant ambivalence among white working-class people—a people without a party.

### What are white working-class policy ideologies and attitudes?

#### United States

In the United States, these partisan trends reflect tectonic shifts in white working-class people's self-reported ideology over time. Despite their once-heavy Democratic identification in the 1960s and 1970s, relatively few white working-class people ever reported liberal political ideologies. So those who shifted their partisan leanings to the Right during the last half-century were overwhelmingly those who once described themselves as Moderate, as displayed in Figure 3.5. While this reflects broader polarization of the American public away from moderate ideologies, centrists among the larger population have more evenly dispersed between liberals and conservatives.

Figure 3.6 reports these findings among white working-class people region by region. The drop in moderate ideology is about as steep as the climb in conservative ideology, most pointedly in the American South and West. In the North and North Central regions, which contain more of the Exasperated, there have been modest rises in liberal ideology too.

It is unclear whether changes in policy attitudes alter political ideology or whether changes in political ideology alter policy attitudes. They are intertwined and

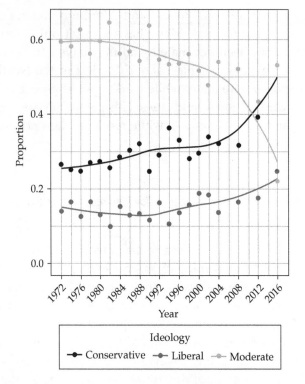

**Figure 3.5** Share of US white working-class adults who identify as a Liberal, Moderate, or Conservative, 1972–2016. Those who said "Don't know" are collapsed into the Moderate category.

*Source*: American National Election Studies cumulative file.

typically move in concert, subject to the influence of political leaders.[1] However, at the core of white working-class Americans' extraordinary evacuation from the Left is their changing view of immigration, and subsequently redistribution. No standardized public opinion data on immigration exist from the 1960s, but there is a categorical difference between the way white working-class people and the rest of the United States have viewed immigration since 1992. As displayed in Figure 3.7, white working-class

**Figure 3.6** Share of US white working-class adults who identify as a Liberal, Moderate, or Conservative by region, 1972–2016. Those who answered "Don't know" are collapsed into the Moderate category.

*Source*: American National Election Studies cumulative file.

people are far more likely to advocate for the reduction of immigration. Other Americans were more likely to express satisfaction with current numbers or desire an increase. During the same time period, white working-class people also reported a consistently worse impression of

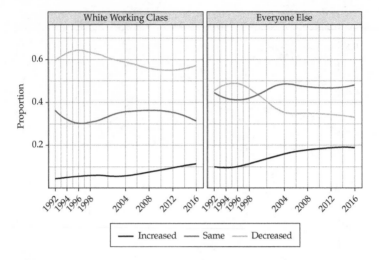

**Figure 3.7** Distribution of responses to "Do you think the number of immigrants from foreign counties who are permitted to come to the United States to live should be increased a lot, increased a little, decreased a little, decreased a lot, or left the same?" among white working-class people and all others.

*Source:* American National Election Studies cumulative data file.

undocumented immigrants, steadily 15 points lower than other Americans over nearly a 30-year span. Despite this gap, as displayed in Figure 3.8, white working-class people have joined a more positive general trend in feelings toward the undocumented.

It is no coincidence that anxiety over immigration is a prominent manifestation of changes in white working-class people's political ideology since the Civil Rights Movement. In 1965, the Lyndon B. Johnson administration eliminated a national origins quota system, which had capped immigration from the Eastern Hemisphere at 170,000, with country-specific maximums, and capped Western Hemisphere immigration at 120,000, with further country-specific quotas added in 1976.[2] Coinciding with decolonization, European countries (along with other

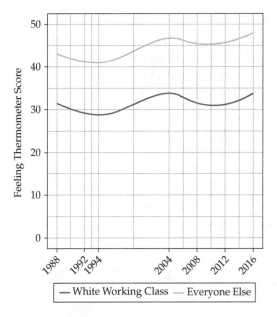

**Figure 3.8** Respondents were asked how they feel about "illegal aliens." Answers range from 0, indicating a very cold or negative feeling toward the group, to 100, indicating a very positive and warm feeling toward the group, 1988–2016.

*Source*: American National Election Studies cumulative data file.

settler states) likewise revised their similarly discriminatory laws. These changes opened the door to the admission of, principally, Africans and South Asians in Europe, and the admission of, principally, Latinos and East Asians in North America ever since. Before 1965, white working-class people were typically the descendants of the most recent waves of American immigrants or immigrants themselves. Their views about immigration evolved as their own immigrant history grew more distant, the composition of American immigrants changed, and people with darker skin were admitted. When immigration policy was made, it was no longer thought to apply to white people.

As the first president with dark skin, Barack Obama's historic election in 2008 marks a further disjuncture. Obama, the son of a Kenyan father, symbolized the demographic change that had taken place in the United States and, for many white Americans, their loosening grip on social order. Consequently, many voters hit the brakes on America's progress toward an alternative future.

Across issue areas since 2008, this reaction has been most visible in white working-class people's attitudes about redistributive policies. As displayed in Figures 3.9, 3.10 and 3.11, white people without university degrees

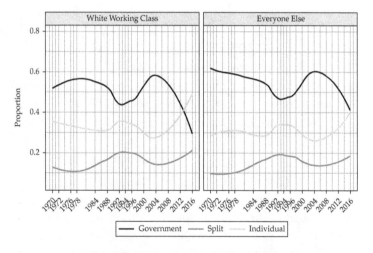

**Figure 3.9** Distribution of responses to "There is much concern about the rapid rise in medical and hospital costs. Some people feel there should be a government insurance plan, which would cover all medical and hospital expenses for everyone. Others feel that all medical expenses should be paid by individuals, and through private insurance plans like Blue Cross. Where would you place yourself on this scale, or haven't you thought much about this?" among white working-class respondents and all others, 1970–2016.

*Source*: American National Election Studies cumulative data file.

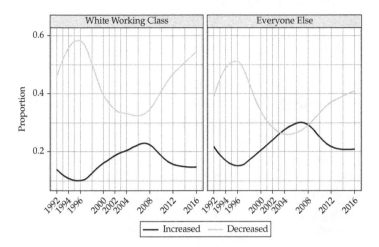

**Figure 3.10** Distribution of responses to "If you had a say in making up the federal budget this year, for which programs would you like to see spending increased and for which would you like to see spending decreased: Should federal spending on welfare be increased, decreased or kept about the same?" among white working-class respondents and all others, 1992–2016.

*Source*: American National Election Studies cumulative data file.

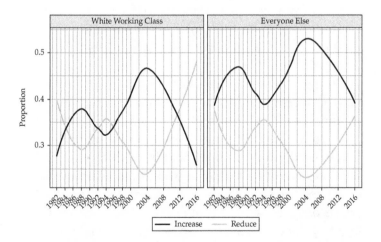

**Figure 3.11** Distribution of responses to "Some people think the government should provide fewer services, even in areas such as health and education in order to reduce spending. Other people feel it is important for the government to provide many more services even if it means an increase in spending. Where would you place yourself on this scale?" among white working-class respondents and all others, 1982–2016.

*Source*: American National Election Studies cumulative data file.

have been less and less supportive of government coordination of health care, government spending on welfare benefits, and government spending more generally. Each of these trends is also true for the American public at large, but with lower magnitude. Each plot of public opinion reveals a clear breaking point around the time of Obama's presidential campaign and election. It is important to acknowledge that this period was also characterized by the onset of the global economic crisis, but white working-class people were the first to feel the pinch of layoffs, cutbacks, and austerity. Despite being a potential beneficiary of government programs that support the poor's basic needs, individualism reigned.

As Americans became poorer, they became less and less inclined to share wealth but also more disdainful of the poor—even when they were poor themselves. As shown in Figure 3.12, the impression of welfare recipients dropped about 10 points during the Obama administration and the recovery from the global economic crisis. However, for the last 30 years, the perception of them among white working-class people has always been about 10 points worse than among the public at large.

During my American fieldwork, many of my interviewees were frustrated by the government's provision of welfare benefits to people they believe are undeserving.[3] They conventionally framed welfare as a matter of morality and dignity—a choice that individuals make when they are unwilling or too lazy to pursue employment— even while many of these respondents accepted welfare provisions themselves to supplement low incomes. A majority of American working-class white people attribute the misfortunes of the poor to their moral worth rather than to structural conditions.[4] In doing so, they draw an unequivocal class boundary between themselves and "the

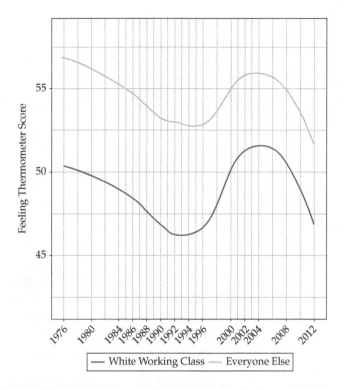

**Figure 3.12** Respondents were asked how they feel about "welfare recipients." Answers range from 0, indicating a very cold or negative feeling toward the group, to 100, indicating a very positive and warm feeling toward the group, 1976–2012.
*Source*: American National Election Studies cumulative data file.

people below" by appealing to an ideal of self-sufficiency. However, many of my interviewees did not believe that such self-sufficiency was valued by their society, which they accused of favoring the pleas of welfare recipients over the silent industry of the working class. Respondents' moralizing pronouncements on welfare align with the general tendency in the United States to distinguish the deserving poor from the undeserving.[5]

This connects to a general perception that "welfare" refers exclusively to cash assistance, rather than food stamps, unemployment, housing, or disability benefits. Given low hourly minimum-wage standards in the United States, cash payments are perceived to rival the incomes of low-wage workers who "work for a living."

A number of researchers argue that there is an ethnocentric inclination among white people to support welfare cuts to people whose income falls below a particular threshold because they disproportionately associate this welfare with black recipients, while social security and job training are associated with white recipients.[6] Welfare operates as a contradictory "symbol of status."[7] Whereas white working-class people view welfare negatively, they also recognize that government support symbolizes a certain badge of respect. The (erroneous) perception that minorities receive governmental support to a greater extent than struggling whites effectively strips working-class white people of their sense of deservingness.

"The minorities that get me are the ones that are uneducated, that realize they have no future, so they get knocked up [pregnant] and collect," one of my American subjects said. "Not all of them do it; many work. But I think that if you're black or Hispanic, you can get almost anything. Meanwhile, I go to the welfare office, and get looked at like 'Why aren't you working?' They come in on drugs and get free food stamps, medical, and unemployment. They know you can only get welfare for a child for the first five years. So they have babies every five years. The squeaky wheel gets all the oil. I've always been one to take care of my own. We're hardworking poor people."

However, because government benefits are perceived to be equally available to white individuals, respondents do not see the social system as structurally discriminatory.

They acknowledge their own capacity to solicit government support.

Rather, they castigate African Americans and Latinos in an effort to establish moral superiority. Unlike their British counterparts, very few of my American interviewees suggested that white Americans are entitled to greater government support than black people. This is partially because many American minorities can compete with white people's claims of heritage, but also because Americans are quicker to acknowledge their own immigrant roots. In light of the fact that their ancestors were once ostracized as immigrants, they view their ancestors' social ascendance past the ranks of African Americans as a matter of personal industriousness, not systemic prejudice.

## United Kingdom

In Britain, white working-class people are bothered by the extension of welfare benefits to immigrants not because they look down upon welfare, but rather because they believe they deserve priority. They typically value National Health Service provisions, public housing, public schools, and other benefits, but they resent that immigrants receive equal standing with British natives in the eyes of the government. Like their American counterparts, they tend to separate themselves from an underclass of others. This has informed a sense of class pride and solidarity that has pervaded East London since the 1930s.

Rather than identify with immigrants' parallel struggle, white working-class people often frame them as competitors for employment and government benefits. Increasingly, they feel displaced by immigrants, not in material terms—working-class whites have always been of modest means and hardly expect that to change—but rather in terms of their place in society. The presence of immigrants has attenuated

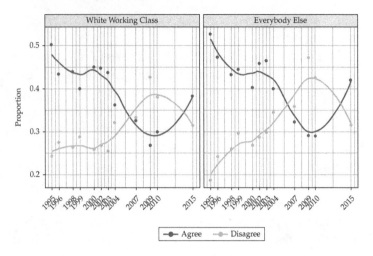

**Figure 3.13** Distribution of UK responses to "Please tell me how much you agree or disagree with the following statement . . . 'The government should spend more money on welfare benefits for the poor, even if it leads to higher taxes' " among white working-class people and everybody else, 1995–2015.
*Source*: British Social Attitudes Survey.

working-class pride, because many white working-class people think that their British authenticity and nationalist sacrifices have been devalued. They sense that they are being pushed to the fringe of British society, where they once placed an underclass of addicts, delinquents, and, indeed, foreigners.

Consequently, many white working-class Britons do not want to throw the baby out with the bathwater. They want to preserve government provisions and end further immigration. Figure 3.13 shows how white working-class people broadly match general British perceptions about whether the government should "spend more money on welfare benefits for the poor, even if it leads to higher taxes." In this context, Figure 3.14 exhibits the greater appeal of class-based populist slogans among white working-class people. At the same time, white working-class Britons

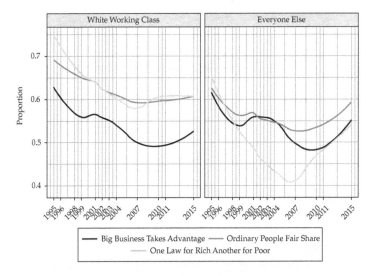

**Figure 3.14** Proportion of people who agree with a series of class-oriented populist statements, including "Big business benefits owners' profit at the expense of workers"; "Ordinary working people do not get their fair share of the nation's wealth"; and "There is one law for the rich and one for the poor"; among white working-class people and everyone else, 1995–2015.
*Source*: British Social Attitudes Survey.

demonstrate the same disdain for people on welfare as do their American counterparts. Figure 3.15 shows that they are consistently harsher than the general population on people who receive government benefits, even though they are likely to be among them. This is because, like Americans, white working-class Britons enjoy a sense of dignity over other people—white or otherwise. Whether it is because they have earned their access to welfare or because they use it legitimately, individuals often distinguish their consumption of government provisions and programs from that of others.

In the eyes of white working-class Britons, immigrants are the least entitled to welfare. They are viewed as exploitative and opportunistic. They are simultaneously blamed

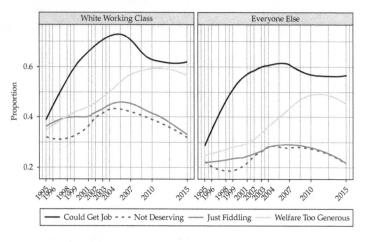

**Figure 3.15**  Proportion of people who agree with a series of derogatory statements about welfare recipients, including: "Around here, most unemployed people could find a job if they wanted"; "Many people who get social security don't really deserve any help"; "Most people on the dole are fiddling in one way or another"; and "If welfare benefits weren't so generous people would learn to stand on their own two feet"; among white working-class people and everybody else, 1995–2015.
*Source*: British Social Attitudes Survey.

for taking British jobs and taking government provisions— ostensibly an impossibility. While one might expect white working-class attitudes toward immigrants in Britain to diverge from the rest of British society, the actual extent is extraordinary in the years they have been measured. Across a number of perceptions about migrant contributions to the British economy (Figure 3.16), migrant contributions to British culture (Figure 3.17), the need for more immigrants (Figure 3.18), and the right of asylum seekers to receive refuge in the United Kingdom (Figure 3.19), white working-class people's attitudes are categorically different. In some cases, they are the complete inverse of the rest of British society.

Immigration-related resentment is likely to also drive categorical differences in perspectives about the European

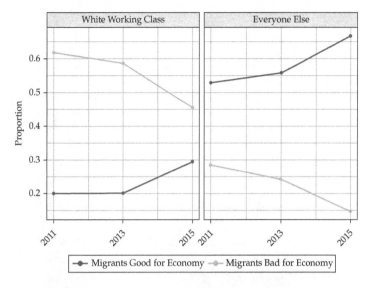

**Figure 3.16** Share of responses to, "On a scale of 0 to 10, where 0 is extremely bad and 10 is extremely good, would you say it is generally bad or good for Britain's economy that migrants come to Britain from other countries?" among white working class and everybody else, 2011–2015. Responses above 5 were coded as "good." *Source*: British Social Attitudes Survey.

Union (Figure 3.20), which guarantees the free movement of people among its member-states. Analyses of the Brexit referendum point to the importance of concerns about immigration among those who voted "Leave." Close to 90 percent of voters who thought that immigration was bad for the economy and voters who thought that immigration should be reduced voted for Brexit.[8] And polls suggest that immigration was the number one issue driving the Leave vote.[9]

Some scholars have pointed to the government's decision not to temporarily restrict immigration from a number of Central and Eastern European countries when they joined the EU in 2004 as "the spark that lit

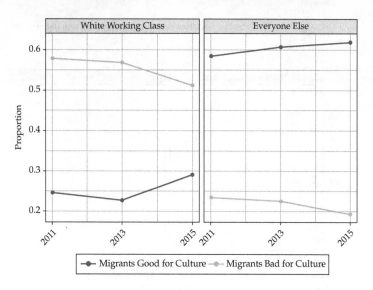

**Figure 3.17** Share of responses to, "On a scale of 0 to 10, would you say that Britain's cultural life is generally undermined or enriched by migrants coming to live here from other countries?" among white working class and everybody else, 2011–2015. Responses above 5 were coded as "good."

*Source*: British Social Attitudes Survey.

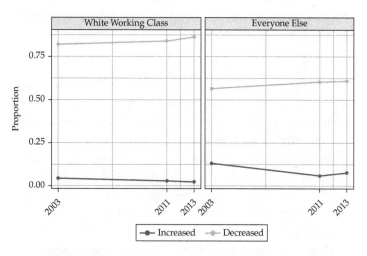

**Figure 3.18** Proportion of people who agree with the statement "Do you think the number of immigrants to Britain nowadays should be increased a lot, increased a little, remain the same as it is, reduced a little or reduced a lot?" among white working-class people and everybody else, 2003–2013.

*Source*: British Social Attitudes Survey.

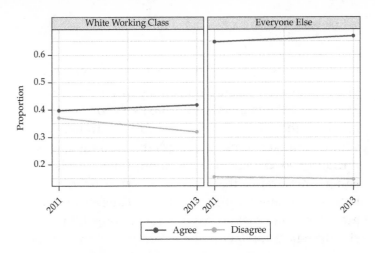

**Figure 3.19** Plotted agree and disagree responses to: "Please tell me how much you agree or disagree with the following statement . . . 'Asylum seekers who have suffered persecution in their own country should be able to stay in Britain?' " among white working-class people and everybody else, 2011–2013. The five-point scale was collapsed into a dichotomous measure of agreement.

*Source*: British Social Attitudes Survey.

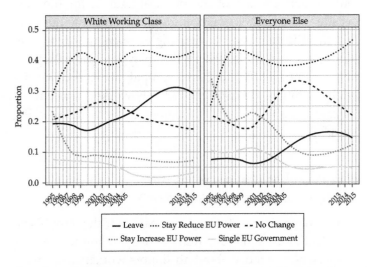

**Figure 3.20** Distribution of responses to "Do you think Britain's long term policy should be to . . ." as it regards UK membership in the European Union, among white working-class people and everybody else, 1995–2015.

*Source*: British Social Attitudes Survey.

this remarkable conflagration."[10] In the Brexit vote, regions with rapid growth in immigration from Eastern European EU members were more likely to vote to leave, although the effect was not particularly strong.[11] It was sudden influxes of new immigrants, creating a sense of uncontrolled change, and not more stable levels of existing immigrants that appear to have driven Leave voters.[12] Although other researchers suggest that immigration did not play as big of a role in Brexit,[13] this may simply reflect the fact that concern over immigration—rather than actual experience with it—motivated many Leave voters.[14]

On balance, immigration consciousness underwent a remarkable transformation in British politics in the decades leading up to the vote. In 1997, only 3 percent of Britons listed immigration as one of the nation's most important issues. By 2007, that figure was over 40 percent and would remain near the top of the political agenda for the next decade.[15] Voters skeptical of immigration came to question Britain's EU membership, creating an opening for the anti-immigration, anti-EU UKIP, which played a lead role in the Brexit campaign.[16] The Leave campaign focused heavily on the immigration issue and actively worked to reach out to traditional Labour areas, bastions of the white working class.[17]

### Do white working-class people consume fewer government resources than others?

During his unsuccessful 1976 campaign for the Republican presidential nomination, Ronald Reagan introduced his supporters to a story about an Illinois woman who made $150,000 a year scamming the welfare system, bringing the term "welfare queen" into the national political dialect.

While the woman in Reagan's story was of ambiguous racial ancestry, the "welfare queen" soon turned into a stereotype of a "lazy black con artist, unashamed of cadging the money that honest folks worked so hard to earn."[18] This image helped create the view that welfare recipients are generally minorities while poor whites work for their living.

Quantitative research has found that the broader American public connects blacks with welfare. Despite dramatic reforms to welfare in the 1990s and changes in views about welfare generally, views on the work ethic of blacks still have a highly significant impact on how likely an individual is to oppose welfare spending.[19] The perception of blacks as greater beneficiaries of welfare is also influenced by media portrayals. One study found that between 1967 and 1992, blacks constituted 57 percent of the portrayals of the poor in major American magazines and television reports, almost double their share of the actual poor.[20] These repeated associations have helped influence the American view that minorities are much more likely to make use of welfare benefits. Britain has a similar stereotype of the exploitative welfare cheat; however, this stereotype is less racialized—the "white version of the black American 'welfare queen.'"[21] Nevertheless, negative views about welfare recipients are pervasive. Forty-three percent of British stories on welfare offered a negative portrayal of the beneficiaries.[22]

The American association between welfare and minorities also extends to immigrants. The prototypical example of the lazy "welfare mother" in a seminal 1975 *New Yorker* article was a Puerto Rican living in New York City.[23] Empirical research has found that concern over immigrants burdening public services is a better explanation of opposition to immigration than concern over competition for jobs.[24] Perhaps the most illustrative manifestation of anger over immigrant use of social services was the passage of Proposition 187 in California in 1994, which banned undocumented immigrants from receiving social services, including health care and public education. Undocumented immigrants are ineligible for conventional welfare programs like cash assistance and food stamps, but the success of this referendum demonstrated a broader view of immigrants as a drain on society. The introduction to Proposition 187 declared that the people of California "have suffered and are suffering economic hardship caused by the presence of illegal immigrants in this state." While the law was largely held unconstitutional by the federal courts, its success demonstrates a public linkage between immigrants and exploitation of government services.

This debate has recently been revived by conservative think tanks. A notable 2015 report by an anti-immigration group argued that immigrants are significantly more likely to use welfare, suggesting that this proves that immigrants are a net burden on society.[25] This study has been debunked for its dramatic exaggeration of immigrant welfare use. It included programs like subsidized school lunches for American citizen children with immigrant parents as "immigrant welfare use."[26] In the American media, though, the initial report garnered significant attention and helped reinforce preexisting beliefs about immigrant welfare use.[27]

Britain has a similar conception of immigrants as "scroungers," coming to exploit the country's generous welfare state.[28] This perception grew rapidly after the 2015 arrival of asylum seekers from across Europe. In advance of the 2016 Brexit vote, Prime Minister David Cameron proposed that new EU immigrants would have to live and work for four years before becoming eligible for British benefits.[29] This measure is remarkably similar to the five-year bar on welfare receipt that was incorporated in America's 1996 welfare reform. This "emergency brake" effort to restrict welfare access to immigrants suggests that, in line with my interviews, welfare itself is not shameful in the United Kingdom, but immigrants' access to it is seen as unfair. Thus, while the perception that minorities and immigrants use a disproportionate share of welfare is not as strong in the United Kingdom as it is in the United States, these views still exist.

On the whole, support for public welfare, or social redistribution, is much more common in Europe. Some scholars attribute a lack of support in the United States in part to America's electoral system, which has helped shut out redistributive parties.[30] However, the United States and the United Kingdom use very similar electoral systems, so this difference cannot explain the gulf in welfare attitudes. Instead, the racial divide in the United States and the greater presence of minorities among the poor have bolstered welfare stereotypes and increased hostility to welfare generally.[31] If racial divides help explain differences in American welfare attitudes, then the rise of xenophobia in Europe can help explain why Britain and the Continent may be turning against welfare too, at least as it is granted to migrants.

The perception that ethnic minorities consume more welfare is not completely divorced from reality. Without accounting for legitimate need, American data suggest that whites are less likely to use welfare. Between 1994 and 1996, non-Hispanic whites in the United States had the lowest participation rate of any major racial or ethnic group in cash assistance, food stamps, Medicaid, and housing assistance. Looking across programs in 1995, over half of American Indians received some form of welfare, as did over 30 percent of non-Hispanic blacks and Hispanics, and fewer than 15 percent of whites.[32] More recent data suggest that these trends continue. Only 15 percent of non-Hispanic white adults have ever received food stamps, compared to 31 percent of non-Hispanic blacks and 22 percent of Hispanics.

However, this differential use of welfare belies differences in poverty rates and other individual-level factors that make someone more likely to need welfare. Between 2007 and 2011, 12 percent of white Americans lived in poverty, compared to 26 percent of African Americans and 23 percent of Hispanics.[33] Non-whites may use welfare more, but they are also needier. Using more advanced statistical techniques, scholars have found that 89 percent of the difference between non-Hispanic whites and blacks in cash benefits receipt can be explained by race-neutral factors like income and family structure and that these factors explain 95 percent of the differences between non-Hispanic whites and Hispanics.[34] After controlling for nonracial factors, race appears to have little to do with how likely Americans are to receive welfare.

Furthermore, despite their lower rates of welfare receipt, non-Hispanic whites receive a greater overall share of food stamps because of their greater numbers in the American population. As of 2013, 40.2 percent of households receiving food stamps are headed by a non-Hispanic white, 25.7 percent by a non-Hispanic African American, and 10.3 percent by a Hispanic person.[35] Similarly, white people make up 71 percent of disability recipients—more than their overall share of the US population—and they receive 16 percent more in average monthly benefits than black recipients.[36]

Whites are also substantially more likely to claim unemployment benefits. Between 1992 and 2010, whites made up 58 percent of the American unemployed but constituted 65 percent of unemployment beneficiaries. In contrast, both Hispanics and non-whites generally constituted a smaller share of beneficiaries relative to their share of the unemployed.[37]

Whites do constitute a minority of cash benefit recipients. In 2013, 27.4 percent of recipients were white, 31.1 percent were black, and 36 percent were Hispanic.[38] However, among adult recipients, white people are actually a slight plurality at 33.3 percent compared to 33.1 percent for blacks and 27.7 percent for Hispanics.[39] While whites use welfare at a lower rate than non-whites in the United States, they still constitute a sizable absolute share if not a majority of all recipients.

Racial disparities in welfare use are less salient in the United Kingdom, perhaps because, even adjusting for their share of the population, whites derive a comparable share of their income from government sources. Overall, white Britons get 15 percent of their income from tax credits, state pensions, and benefits compared with 13 percent for those of mixed ethnicity, 14 percent for Asians, and 18 percent for blacks.[40] While this may be in part due to the share of white Britons receiving state pensions, and the relative youth of immigrant ethnic groups, the similar overall reliance on the state for income across ethnic groups may explain why ethnic differences in welfare receipt are less salient in the United Kingdom.

The 1996 welfare reform in the United States disqualified new documented immigrants from accessing most federal welfare programs for five years and all undocumented immigrants for welfare.[41] Many states have elected to extend state benefits to documented immigrants even though the 1996 reform gave states the authority to deny benefits to immigrants.[42] During the 1980s, when the controversy over immigrant usage of social services was first emerging, researchers looking at Mexican immigrants to California found that "the average cyclical immigrant pays about $200 to $400 more in taxes than he or she uses in services."[43] This study includes services like public education and emergency-room care that fall outside of conventional definitions of "welfare."

Other scholars, like George Borjas and his coauthors, have found that immigrants to the United States are more likely to use welfare, even after controlling for other characteristics.[44] However, these studies took place before the introduction of the 1996 welfare reform. In 2002, Borjas observed that immigrant welfare use dropped off more quickly than native use after the 1996 reform, although he attributes this primarily to the large decline in welfare use in California after 1996.[45]

In Britain, welfare participation by immigrants varies considerably across country of origin. Immigrants from North America, Oceania, and new EU member-states in Central and Eastern Europe are the least likely to claim welfare, perhaps because they have shorter stays in the United Kingdom. By contrast, immigrants from Asia and the rest of Europe are more likely to receive welfare. In scope, fears of intra-EU migration burdening the welfare system are unfounded.[46] A Parliamentary report affirms these findings, reporting that only 7.2 percent of total Department of Welfare and Pensions benefits claimants were non-UK nationals when they first registered and that non-UK nationals are less likely than natives to receive unemployment benefits.[47]

Placing American and British trends in context, one of the broadest studies of Europe found that after controlling for individual characteristics, immigrants to Germany,

Britain, Greece, Spain, and Portugal are as likely or less likely to access welfare than natives, while in Denmark, the Netherlands, Belgium, France, Austria, and Finland, immigrants are significantly more likely to access welfare. This divergence suggests that the relationship between immigration and welfare receipt is not uniform across countries and that national institutions play an important role.[48]

### Are white working-class people losing jobs to immigrants and minority groups?

In his July 2016 speech at the Republican National Convention, Donald Trump declared that "decades of record immigration have produced lower wages and higher unemployment for our citizens, especially for African-American and Latino workers."[49] In an earlier speech, Trump left out the appeal to African Americans and Latinos, but made a similar argument about Mexicans: "They're taking our jobs. They're taking our manufacturing jobs. They're taking our money. They're killing us."[50] While muddling whether he was referring to Mexican immigrants or Mexicans in Mexico, Trump made explicit a long-standing argument in American politics: immigrants take American jobs.[51]

Even President George W. Bush, known for his support of comprehensive immigration reform, repeated this argument, albeit more subtly. He repeatedly emphasized that his proposed guest worker program was only for jobs that Americans had not taken and that American workers needed to be prioritized,[52] acknowledging the fear that immigrants cause native job loss.

Trump's remarks also highlight the linkage between competition for jobs and wages. If immigrants are willing to work for less than natives would, they can undercut native wages or replace natives altogether. This argument is often targeted specifically against undocumented workers,[53] who can sometimes be exploited to work for less pay than native workers would receive and who are reluctant to appeal to regulators about substandard work conditions or pay. Because of this, some observers argue that immigrants undercut the labor market and "take" jobs even if native workers would not be willing to do the work at that wage.

Similar claims that immigrants take native jobs have been made in the United Kingdom, particularly during the Brexit campaign. The UKIP leader, Nigel Farage, claimed that new EU immigrants were driving down wages for native Britons.[54] Farage also claimed more boldly (and incorrectly) that 80 percent of new jobs created in Britain were taken by immigrants.[55] This rhetoric has continued even after the Brexit vote. Amanda Rudd, Prime Minister May's Home Secretary, declared at an October 2016 Conservative Party conference that she would toughen labor-market testing to "ensure people coming here are filling gaps in the labor market, not taking jobs British people could do."[56]

This rhetoric of "taking" jobs is also targeted at minorities because of affirmative action. Though often associated with university admissions, affirmative action is also frequently used in hiring and contracting. Some have attacked the programs as "neosocialism," hurting the economy by putting quotas over merit.[57] In this narrative, deserving whites are being superseded by presumptively less qualified minorities.

One poll found the practice was supported by only 46 percent of white Americans compared to 75 percent of black Americans.[58] Eight states, including traditionally left-wing regions like California and Washington, have an executive order, law, or constitutional amendment banning affirmative action by public institutions, including in employment.[59] Most of these bans were adopted by voters at the ballot box, largely by initiative,[60] suggesting widespread popular opposition to the practice.

In the United Kingdom, employment-based affirmative action (also called positive action) is less controversial. The Equality Act of 2010 specifically prohibits any preferential treatment in employment on the basis of race.[61] Affirmative action is permitted in hiring and promotion only as a tiebreaker between equally qualified applicants and is subject to a number of additional restrictions.[62] The Equality Act is framed in broad terms, encompassing sex, race, disability, age, sexual orientation, and a number of other categories. Because of the equal qualification requirement, the voluntary nature of the program, and the fact that nonracial minorities have the potential to benefit, positive action in Britain has stirred far less controversy than affirmative action in the United States.

The relationship between immigration and native employment is difficult to test. Because the number of jobs in an economy is not fixed, an individual job cannot be "taken" from a white person. If a position that would have otherwise gone to a citizen is filled by an immigrant, that immigrant has more money, increasing aggregate demand and helping to create additional jobs that could be filled by the native-born, immigrants, or people in other countries. The interrelation of this process therefore makes this an area with few clear answers. Population growth increases both the number of workers and the number of jobs.[63] Because the job market is not a zero-sum game, immigrants can "take" native jobs while creating even more jobs for everyone.

Moreover, skilled immigrants can open new businesses, file patents, foster innovation, and create jobs for native-born workers directly. Thus, even if the native-born are replaced by immigrants, they may find new work in a business that was created by another immigrant. Because of this, the effect of immigration varies based on the skill level of immigration flows. Preliminary evidence suggests that immigrants file more patents per capita than natives each year, but these data are not sufficient to demonstrate a direct effect in the net number of jobs.[64]

Empirical research highlights these ambiguities. A study found that in the United States, "no consistent pattern emerges to show that native-born workers suffered or benefited from increased numbers of foreign-born workers."[65] That study found that, in 2000, 25 percent of native-born workers lived in states with rapid immigrant population growth and favorable economic outcomes for natives, 15 percent lived in states with rapid immigrant population growth and negative economic outcomes for natives, and 60 percent lived in states with below-average immigrant population growth.[66] What this variation demonstrates is that the impact of immigration on native-born workers is ambiguous at best. Even the conservative economist George Borjas, who has written about the negative effect of immigration on native wages,[67] acknowledges that immigration has little effect on native labor-force participation at the local level, although he argues that research is still unclear at the national level.[68]

A comprehensive September 2016 report, assembled by an ideologically diverse group of American economists and sociologists, including Borjas, sought to evaluate the cumulative effect of immigration on the American economy.[69] These scholars argued that while many will be unaffected by immigration, preexisting workers, including prior immigrants, could be negatively impacted depending on the size, speed, and skill level of new immigration flows.[70] Ultimately, though, untangling the effects of immigration on the labor market is challenging because it is impossible to know which wages and employment outcomes would have occurred without immigration.[71] They conclude that the effect of immigration on employment is "complex and difficult to measure."[72]

Despite these difficulties, these scholars did reach some conclusions. For example, they note that because competition for jobs goes hand-in-hand with increased immigrant spending, immigration has only a small impact on wages.[73] These effects are particularly small when viewed over a time frame of 10 years or more.[74] Despite these small effects, a consensus exists that those workers who hold jobs that are most likely to be filled by new immigrants are the most vulnerable to wage declines. Those most likely to experience these negative effects are prior immigrants, followed by native-born Americans without a high school degree.[75] In particular, native-born ethnic minorities may bear the brunt of immigration more than whites.[76] Thus, even if immigration has a negative effect on native workers, that does not mean that it is the white working class that is losing out.

Results on high-skilled immigration are more mixed. Some studies find that high-skilled immigration boosts the wages and employment of natives, but others find that high-skilled immigration in narrow fields (like professional mathematics) can hurt the employment prospects of natives in that field.[77] Research showing that high-skilled immigrants tend to be innovators suggests a potential positive effect on employment for white working-class people.

The growth in immigration has also occurred simultaneously with new trends in globalization, including international trade and outsourcing.[78] If these structural changes—and not immigration—are the root cause of employment effects, immigrants may be scapegoated for changes that reach far beyond their decision to migrate. Some have blamed technological advances that automate

tasks for poor job growth since the turn of the millen-
nium.[79] The simultaneous occurrence of these trends, all
of which have the potential to negatively impact native
employment, not only makes it difficult for observers to
disentangle the relative contributions of these effects but
also makes it easy for politicians to blame immigrants for
outcomes that might properly be attributed to complicated
transnational forces and decisions made by domestic elites.

Research from Europe suggests that immigration
can actually help native workers, encouraging them to
take on more skilled employment while leaving lower-
paying manual tasks for new immigrants.[80] Because white
working-class people often have superior language and
communication skills relative to new immigrants, immigration can help restructure the labor market and boost the
wages of native whites.

Findings from Britain also suggest that working-class
whites are not losing out to immigrants. At the local level,
areas with higher employment rates for foreigners also
had higher employment rates for white native Britons.[81]
More generally, the British unemployment rate fell below
5 percent in 2016, close to a historic low,[82] just as Brexit
campaigners were ratcheting up anti-immigration rhetoric.
Even if immigrants were taking British jobs, there were
relatively few unemployed Britons to fill these positions
anyway. While results are mixed on non-EU migrants, the
claims about EU migrants that help fueled Brexit appear to
largely be false. Most researchers find that EU migrants to
the United Kingdom do not take jobs from native Britons.

Despite rhetoric against affirmative action, little schol-
arly evidence exists to suggest that white people are
losing out on employment due to these policies. In fact,
affirmative action may promote an attitude toward hiring
that encourages employers to look beyond preexisting
networks, to which white working-class people may not
be privy either. In this spirit, companies are becoming

increasingly conscious of including people with different socioeconomic statuses. And despite dislike for affirmative action in the abstract, when asked if they think they themselves were denied a job or promotion because of their race, the vast majority of white people say no—88 percent to 95 percent across different estimates.[83] Overall, scholars conclude that more people fear affirmative action than are actually harmed by it.[84] Affirmative action appears to be less of a threat to white working-class employment than opponents make it out to be.

### What drives white working-class tolerance and intolerance of ethnic minorities?

Hillary Clinton's comment that "you could put half of Trump's supporters into what I call the basket of deplorables"[85] helped inject a debate about the intolerance of working-class whites directly into the 2016 American election. In her comments, Clinton identified the members of this basket as "the racist, sexist, homophobic, xenophobic, Islamophobic—you name it."[86] While her remarks drew criticism and indeed she later admitted the estimate was a "gross generalization," her claims about the extent of prejudice may not have been that far from reality. The polling firm YouGov evaluates respondents' beliefs about race through a standard battery of questions on preferential treatment of minorities instead of asking about racial beliefs directly. They found that 58 percent of Trump supporters fell in the top quartile of those Americans expressing racial resentment and that 91 percent beat the national median.[87] While the term "deplorable" was highly charged and offensive to many white working class people, her estimate of racial resentment among Trump supporters was not that far off the mark.

The United States and United Kingdom both witnessed spikes in hate crimes after their 2016 elections. In the 10 days after President Trump's election, the Southern

Poverty Law Center documented 867 hate incidents.[88] Britain saw reported hate crimes rise 57 percent in the four days after the Brexit vote.[89] The Equality and Human Rights Commission called the spike "unprecedented."[90] While this level of violence may be unprecedented, racism and anti-immigrant sentiment are not.

A rich research tradition in political science and sociology dating back to the 1940s[91] attempts to explain why groups fail to get along. The political scientist Benjamin Newman underscores the pace of demographic change as a key determinant for intolerance in the United States.[92] He identifies differences between communities that experience a rapid influx of immigrants and those that have already experienced more gradual change and acculturation. Rapid changes can lead to resentment among existing majorities, but more incremental change is less likely to incite a backlash. This theory builds on older research on black-white relations, which argued that a sudden influx of minorities to a white neighborhood could fuel an antiminority crime wave.[93]

Since 1970, the number of immigrants in the United States has more than quadrupled,[94] and since 1993, the number of immigrants in the United Kingdom has more than doubled.[95] These rapid shifts could help explain why anti-immigrant sentiment has emerged so prominently in both countries in recent years. These findings undermine earlier understandings, according to which intolerance increases as the immigrant population grows larger because of greater political and economic competition between natives and nonnatives.[96]

This "pace of change" theory also focuses on the uncertainty and fear of nonassimilation that rapid change can bring. It builds on older theories of "cultural threat," which argue that prejudice against immigrants is driven by a perceived threat to national cultural identity. The cultural threat explanation has largely trumped economic explanations. Research found that in the United States[97] and Europe,[98] concerns over cultural changes dwarfed personal economic factors in driving anti-immigrant and anti-immigration sentiment. On the whole, attitudes toward immigration have little correlation with individual economic factors and are more shaped by national-level concerns.[99]

This research also builds on "contact" theories, which contend that, in areas with large shares of immigrants already, contact between groups promotes tolerance.[100] Opposing "conflict" theories argue that frequent intergroup interactions actually lead to competition, enhancing animosity. A large-scale analysis of more than 500 studies found greater evidence for the validity of contact theory,[101] although other scholars argue that results are generally inconsistent.[102] On the whole though, there appears to be an emerging consensus that close interaction with minorities should, in general, help promote tolerance. The problem is that many post-traumatic cities and new immigration destinations are subject to significant residential segregation. Working-class white people saw enough of minorities to be alarmed by the rapid changes in their communities, but they did not actually live close enough to interact with them and develop empathy and mutual understanding.

Recent studies propose more complicated relationships. Some scholars find that the effect of close interaction with minorities varies depending on the group. One study, for example, found that non-Hispanic whites in the United States were more likely to have positive attitudes about immigrants if they lived near Asians and more likely to have negative attitudes about immigrants if they lived near Hispanics.[103] Others argue that the relationship between minority interaction is parabolic. Small numbers of minorities are not threatening, but when group size grows, so does intolerance. When that minority begins to become a majority in that area, though, the former majority may grow more comfortable with them.[104]

Residential segregation alone also cannot explain the rapid increase in racial salience during the Obama administration. While the history of this era has yet to be written, preliminary research suggests that Barack Obama's election to the presidency and the perceived increase in power of African Americans that accompanied it increased racial resentment among whites. One study found that "priming" respondents with a reminder of President Obama's election as a racial milestone increased implicit bias.[105] However, other scholars have found a positive "Obama effect" where his election decreased negative stereotypes among whites about blacks.[106] Thus, it is possible that recent racial tensions are not the result of increasing intolerance, but an activation of preexisting fears.

In line with the research on President Obama's election, other research finds that even small interactions with minorities increase antiminority sentiment. The political scientist Ryan Enos placed Spanish-speaking people near Boston commuters and observed a statistically significant decrease in support for immigration among people who were near the Spanish speakers when they were offered the survey.[107] This research tends more toward the conflict theory and suggests that, at the individual level, the close presence of minorities does not produce immediate empathy and understanding. Instead, latent biases might be activated when there is interaction—but no engagement—with minorities.

The political scientist Joel Olson framed these relationships in even starker terms. During slavery and segregation, he wrote, "white identity functioned as a form of racialized standing that granted all whites a superior status to all those who were not white. . . . The loss of individualized standing due to the victories of the civil rights movement, however, led to anger, anxiety, and resentment among whites, and a desire to restore that standing."[108] Many researchers believe that it is this base desire that has driven trends in political attitudes ever since.

# 4

# WHITE WORKING-CLASS
# PEOPLE AND VOTING

*What are white working-class voting trends over time?*

The Clinton presidency and Blair government marked parallel pivots in the trajectory of the Democratic and Labour parties—a pursuit of what has been termed a "Third Way." Since the 1930s, the parties had been associated with unionism, worker protections, social welfare, and protectionist stances on trade. They were skeptical of foreign interventionism during the Cold War, prioritizing "butter" over "guns." However, in an embrace of the economic and social globalization that infused the spirit after the fall of the Berlin Wall, Clinton and Blair aligned their parties more closely with the financial class of Wall Street and the City of London. In the United States, this was also in recognition of Democrats' need to compete for fundraising dollars. And after humanitarian actions in the Balkans, East Timor, and sub-Saharan Africa (along with Blair's complicity in Iraq), little differentiated the globalism of the Left from the globalism of the Right. Rather, the Left and Right became more distinct in their differing social values related to race, immigration, sexuality, religion, guns (in the United States), and the European Union (in Britain). The Left's white working-class constituency took notice.

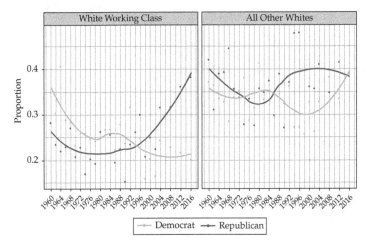

**Figure 4.1** Self-reported vote for Democratic or Republican House of Representatives candidates among the white working class and all other whites, 1960–2016.
*Source*: American National Election Studies cumulative data file.

In the United States, a stunning reversal of voting patterns has taken place since the early 1990s. White working-class voters turned their backs on the Democratic Party, which many feel turned its back on them. Figures 4.1 and 4.2 illustrate the extraordinary shift over the last 40 years. Among white working-class people reporting their votes for local representatives and presidential candidates, the share supporting Republicans nearly doubled in size. During the same period, the Democratic Party made steady gains in support from white voters with university degrees, and nearly monopolized support from ethnic minorities. Examining the shift in Republican support among white working-class people and all other white people from the 2012 to the 2016 election, I find that more white working-class people voted for Donald Trump than Mitt Romney in 42 out of 50 states. And of these 42 states, more white working-class people shifted to the Republican Party than

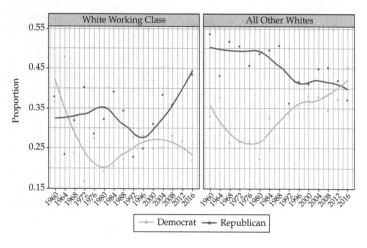

**Figure 4.2** Self-reported vote for Democratic or Republican presidential candidates among the white working class and all other whites, 1960–2016.
*Source*: American National Election Studies cumulative data file.

other white voters in all states except Delaware and (only barely) Vermont. Approximately 10 percent increases took place in Rust Belt states like Wisconsin, Indiana, Michigan, and Pennsylvania.

Examining actual presidential election voting patterns in Figure 4.3, the trajectory is even starker. After an approximate 50-50 split of white working-class votes between Bill Clinton and Republican Bob Dole in 1996, Hillary Clinton lost this constituency to Donald Trump by a three-to-one ratio. In the 660 predominantly white working-class counties nationwide identified in Chapter 1, Hillary Clinton won a mere two. Without making any compromises in their economic and fiscal agenda, the Republican Party has redefined its principal constituency.

In the United Kingdom, recent election cycles have been distorted by the ephemeral presence of the Brexit-rallying United Kingdom Independence Party (UKIP). In 2015, they

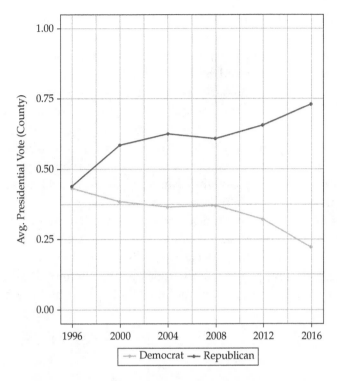

**Figure 4.3** Average vote for Democratic and Republican presidential candidates in US counties that are over 85 percent white and under median national income, 1996–2016.

*Source*: Congressional Quarterly Voting and Elections Data Collection.

were backed by a substantial number of voters who had previously supported Labour, the Liberal Democrats, or sat out, bolstering the Conservative Party to victory in much of England (Figure 4.4). Although UKIP's 13 percent of the popular vote only yielded one Parliamentary seat, their momentum carried into the 2016 Brexit referendum. After the successful "Leave" campaign, UKIP's purpose became unclear. The party had what was effectively a single-issue platform—a halt to immigration, encapsulated by their advocacy for Britain's departure from the European Union. Once that took place, the mobilization of their voters waned. Their leader, Nigel Farage, stepped down, infighting commenced, and their only Member of Parliament resigned from the party in April 2017. In the 2017 election the party won no seats and saw its vote share plummet from 13 percent to less than 2 percent (See Figure 4.4).[1]

In the 2017 snap election called by Prime Minister Theresa May, Labour declared the hung Parliament result a victory in light of the seats they recovered. However, strong signs point to Labour's survival as an chimera that is not attributable to their divisive leader, Jeremy Corbyn. In particular, Labour benefited from three factors.

First, in holding an election so swiftly after the Brexit referendum, pro-Remain voters were highly mobilized to turn out to reject the Conservative Party pursuing Britain's

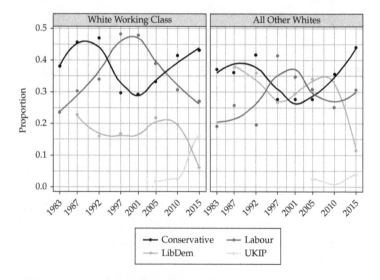

**Figure 4.4** Self-reported vote for Conservative, Labour, Liberal Democrat, and UKIP candidates among the white working class and all other whites, 1983–2015.
*Source:* British Election Study.

departure. Second, the prime minister ran, by nearly all accounts, a historically unpersuasive campaign that was haunted by the absence of any accomplishments or clear direction in Brexit negotiations. There was little to vote for beyond stability. And third, Labor increased its vote share to 40 percent from 29 percent after the 2010 election, but it had only four more seats to show for it. The party merely deepened its coalition in the regions where it had already been strong; it is not expanding to reach white working-class voters or other constituencies. The future of British partisanship depends on the results of the Brexit negotiation, on the resuscitation of the Radical Right, and on Labour's appetite for reconnecting with its lost base.

### Why do white working-class people support Donald Trump and Radical Right parties?

The Radical Right constitutes an extreme on an ideological spectrum characterized by xenophobia, racial resentment, nationalism, isolationism, and otherwise authoritarian tendencies.[2] There is a Radical Right party or movement in nearly every European country today and, in the politics and rhetoric of President Trump, the United States has its own expression. Three classes of "protests" explain the emergence of the Radical Right: economic, political, and social.[3]

Economically, scores of studies in the world's democracies have found a strong link between economic conditions and electoral outcomes. Scholars find that voters are more likely to support parties in power during periods of economic growth. When growth stagnates, voters remove them from power.[4] According to this perspective, support for Radical Right candidates and parties can be understood as a response to larger macroeconomic trends and the global economic collapse since 2008.[5] In postindustrial regions of the United States and Europe, the collapse was precipitated first by the swift dismantling of manufacturing sectors and the rise of privatization and supply-side economics.[6] Each of these trends had a disproportionate effect on middle- and low-skilled workers.[7] During this period, Radical Right parties and candidates have crafted narratives that portray the political establishment as, at best, incompetent or, at worst, culpable for conspiring against the interests of the working classes.[8]

Politically, this sense of conspiracy reflects a more pervasive sense of powerlessness among supporters of the Radical Right. The Radical Right has profited from frustrations about EU integration, political corruption scandals,[9] and politicians perceived to be out of touch with the needs of average people.[10] In Europe, parties who appeal to these sentiments have been particularly successful in electoral systems that feature proportional representation, which grants fringe parties parliamentary representation and power in the formation of coalitions.[11] In both the United States and Europe, the greater sense of powerlessness relates to shifts in partisan alignment. Many Radical Right supporters were once fervent members of the mainstream Left, which was variably anchored by unionism, protectionism, and a base of working-class white voters.[12] In America, the transition of the FDR-LBJ Democratic Party to its modern coalition of urban liberals, minority groups, and what remains of labor organizations has been understood as a matter of rights and identity politics,[13] the rise of Wall Street's influence,[14] and the rapid decline in union power.[15] In Britain, since Tony Blair and New Labour turned away from the party's socialist roots, it has been decimated by the loss of white working-class support and internal debates over immigration, identity politics, and foreign interventionism.

Socially, researchers have contended that support for the Radical Right is mobilized by a sense of social or cultural threat that overrides economic and political grievances. In the American context, the paranoia of the American Far Right is thought to be a reaction to a perceived drops in (or threats to) whites' social status as a result of social change.[16] The political reaction to such change is often an "all-out crusade" to stop the forces of progress.[17] Following this line of reasoning, Chris Parker and Matt Barreto have argued that the post-2008 groundswell of support for the Tea Party is similar to support for the Radical Right in other periods of American history, including the Ku Klux Klan in the 1920s and the John Birch Society in the 1960s. This more recent anxiety is triggered not by a burgeoning Civil Rights Movement but by the accumulation of immigrant flows and the election of the first African American president. In this vein, scholars have noted that Donald Trump's support is strongest among those concerned about social and demographic change, expressed in the form of racism,[18] ethnocentrism and xenophobia,[19] and authoritarianism.[20]

A similar focus on social and cultural threat has characterized research in European countries, where the Radical Right rejects multiculturalism and European integration, appealing to xenophobia and racism.[21] This has resonated as the immigration of non-white or non-Christian people increases. Concerns about national identity dominate economic concerns in sparking anti-immigrant reactions.[22] Accordingly, anti-immigration appeals— not political or economic appeals—are thought to unite support behind successful populist parties in Europe.[23] The bulk of scientific evidence suggests that such attitudes are mostly driven by symbolic concerns about the nation and identity.[24]

For many individuals, immigration and demographic change pose a visible and direct threat to established concepts of nation, identity, and social hierarchies. Over the course of American history, Cheryl Harris argued, "the set of assumptions, privileges, and benefits that accompany the status of being white have become a valuable asset that whites sought to protect."[25] Harris referred to these assumptions, privileges, and benefits as the "settled expectations of whiteness." Others approach this whiteness as a "glass floor below which the white citizen could see but never fall."[26] While such standing did not guarantee white working-class people prosperity, it rendered relative advantage to blacks—a sort of consolation prize related to what W. E. B. Du Bois called the "psychological wages of whiteness."[27]

These settled expectations are passed down through generations such that individuals expect to meet or exceed the living standards of their parents' generation.[28] White people working and raising families throughout the latter half of the twentieth century enjoyed a measure of economic mobility,[29] an era of unprecedented political cohesion,[30] and social dominance.[31] Indeed, a central tenet of the American Dream is that each generation will do better than the previous generation. These settled expectations have become so embedded, they are understood by whites as "a natural order of things that cannot legitimately be disturbed."[32]

With recent transformations of the global economy, Western demography, and subsequent political decisions by governing elites, white people in North America and Europe experienced a change from a system in which they directed most governing institutions to one based on legal guarantees of equal rights.[33] While this understanding of racial politics emerges from the American experience, it may be extended to Europe in light of the economic and demographic changes that both continents have undergone and the rigid racial hierarchy that has long defined both.

Building on this substantial foundation, my own research contends that those who support the Radical Right are primarily driven by a perceived threat to a loss of status over time—a nostalgic sense of social, political, or economic deprivation. This "nostalgic deprivation" is measurable in the discrepancies between where people see their current social position, financial well-being, and political power and where they believe they stood on all of these points a generation earlier. The greater the loss of status the individual perceives, the more likely the individual is to support a Radical Right candidate or party.

Figure 4.5 displays the percentage of the people from nationally representative samples of white people from the United States and the United Kingdom who feel more deprived, no different, and less deprived relative to people like them 30 years ago in social standing, economic well-being,

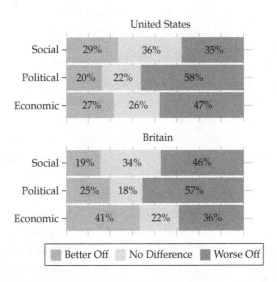

**Figure 4.5** The proportion of white adults in the United States and Britain who perceive themselves to be less deprived (left), no different (middle), or more deprived (right) in terms of social, political, or economic centrality over time.

and political power. Between a third and a half of white adults in both countries perceive themselves becoming of lower status in one domain. Looking at social standing, 35 percent of white Americans feel socially demoted today compared to 30 years ago. The same goes for 46 percent of the sample in Britain. An even larger percentage believe they have lost political power over the last 30 years, or that politicians care less about them than they did 30 years ago. Nearly 6 in 10 white adults in both countries feel that they have lost political power. Finally, a larger proportion of white Americans, nearly half, feel that they are less financially well off than people like them 30 years ago. Only 36 percent of white adults feel the same way in Britain. These findings highlight the general sense of backsliding that many perceive in an era of globalization, migration, gridlock, and increasing economic inequality.

This "nostalgic deprivation" is a strong predictor of voting behavior, particularly among conservatives. Given the increase in people's sense of deprivation, I measured the change in the predicted probability of support for UKIP and the British National Party in Britain, and for the Tea Party and Donald Trump in the United States on a zero-to-one scale. I conducted these surveys a year before the Brexit referendum (May 2015 in the United Kingdom) and nearly a year before Donald Trump's election victory (December 2015 in the United States); at the time, support for Trump's candidacy was around 30 percent nationally within the Republican field.[34]

Controlling for factors including people's partisanship, age, education, gender, home ownership, and marital status, I found that, among self-identified Republicans, nostalgic deprivation was a strong determinant of support for the Radical Right. A sense of economic deprivation increased support for the Tea Party by 0.15 points and for Donald Trump by 0.41 points; perceived political deprivation increased support for the Tea Party by 0.20 and for

Donald Trump by 0.23; and perceived social deprivation increased support for the Tea Party by 0.26 but does not appear to be associated with increased support for Donald Trump. Given that each outcome was scaled between 0 and 1, these effects are very large. The results suggest that it is not just economic concerns among Republicans that drive support for the Tea Party, but social and political concerns, a feeling that the country and political system are being taken over by out-groups at the expense of the in-group. Support for Trump among Republicans appears to be driven by perceived economic and political deprivation.

For Democrats, the effect of nostalgic deprivation is largely null or negative. Democrats who perceive themselves to be most deprived are consistently less likely to support the Radical Right. Finally, the results for Independents are mixed. In most cases, nostalgic deprivation has no effect on Independent support for the Radical Right, except that perceived economic deprivation is positively associated with support for Trump. This is consistent with Trump's victories in economically depressed regions like the Rust Belt and Appalachia, where many Democrats who left their party were mobilized by his economic populist message. This demonstrates how Trump voters in 2016 were more diverse than many recognize, comprising people with different motivations in some regions and living conditions and quite different motivations in others.

Overall, two important findings emerged in the US survey data. First, perceived political deprivation appears to be a consistent and strong determinant of support for the Radical Right among Republicans in the United States. When Republican respondents believe that the political system no longer cares about people like them, they tend to look to more radical alternatives, whether it be a grassroots small-government movement like the Tea Party or a nationalist strong-man like Trump. Second, the differential impacts of perceived social and economic deprivation on support for the Tea Party and Trump respectively highlight the different strains of Radical Right support in the United States. The Tea Party movement is driven more by perceived social and political change than perceived economic hardship.

In the United Kingdom, nostalgic deprivation has a significant impact on support for Radical Right parties, particularly UKIP, among Conservatives. (British surveys did not classify some voters as "Independents.") Perceived economic deprivation increased support for UKIP by 0.30 points, social deprivation by 0.20 points, and political deprivation by a remarkable 0.82 points. As with the American sample, perceived political deprivation appears to have the largest impact on support for the Radical Right in Britain, followed by economic and social deprivation. Also, similar to the United States, there appear to be null or negative associations between nostalgic deprivation among Labour voters and support for the Radical Right. The one exception is that Labour members who are politically deprived are marginally more likely to support UKIP than those who are not politically deprived. In many ways, UKIP harvested political capital among alienated unionists and leftists who felt like the Labour Party abandoned their interests after aligning with London's cosmopolitan financial class and ethnic minorities. In sum, nostalgic deprivation is a powerful moderator of support for the Radical Right among Conservatives in the United Kingdom, and Republicans and Independents in the United States.

### Will Trumpism outlast Donald Trump?

Throughout the 2016 American presidential campaign, moderates and members of the Republican establishment hoped that Trumpism would turn out to be the brief, dramatic story of a celebrity sweeping up primary voters with lavish but empty promises, and that his harsh "America First" worldview would disappear once it was no longer being flogged from a private jet by a billionaire TV star.[35] Since his victory, those same stalwarts continue to hope that Trump will either moderate his views or that the popularity of his Far Right agenda will diminish among the most fervent members of the Republican base. Some suspected that this might happen as Trumpism is confronted by the practicalities of governance, by the compromises required to pass legislation, or by the follies of simple trial and error.

My research suggests that the dream that Trumpism will die with Donald Trump is just that—a dream. While studying white people's support for the Tea Party and Donald Trump, I also solicited survey respondents' interest in a hypothetical American version of the British National Party (BNP)—the militant Radical Right party that also made a play for British Parliamentary seats in the 2000s. I asked people to imagine that there was a third party in the United States, dedicated to "stopping mass immigration, providing American jobs to American workers, preserving America's Christian heritage, and stopping the threat of Islam"—an American adaptation of the BNP's platform. I asked a nationally representative sample of white people "Would you consider supporting such a party?" A remarkable 65 percent of these respondents said "yes." Clearly, Trump's allure is bigger than Trump himself.

Who would the new party's supporters be? What I found in the study is that, much like those who support Trump, those who would consider voting for this third party are more likely to be male, of lower socioeconomic status, without a university education, and ideologically conservative—in other words, the Republican Party's base. They are also more likely to be young (under 40 years old)—so this is not a phenomenon likely to pass quickly.

It is worth putting the results into perspective. This kind of theoretical question, untethered to any specific party or political figure, may well be a useful test of deep support for such policy platforms. But it is also an imaginary third party right now, free of the media checks and public scrutiny that would accompany it were it to exist in a competitive party landscape. In Britain, for example, UKIP and its precursor, the British National Party, are both stained by allegations of racism and incompetence, while this hypothetical American counterpart is unexposed. But neither the BNP nor UKIP has ever garnered anywhere close to a majority of the white British electorate, let alone a general majority. Sixty-five percent is a whopping number—in fact, it's significantly more than those who expressed support for Trump's candidacy at the time of my research.

It is clear that "nostalgic deprivation" also drives those who would consider supporting this hypothetical Radical Right party in the United States. Perceived economic deprivation increases support for the third party by 0.26 points, perceived political deprivation increases support for the third party by 0.39 points, and perceived social deprivation increases support for the third party by 0.15 points. These are powerful clues that exhibit the way that a perceived drop in status over time is driving the politics of white conservatives in the United States.

As with nearly all presidents before him, Donald Trump's voters are not as likely to mobilize like this in the 2018 midterm election. However, there are two key differences between Trumpism and his UKIP counterparts in Britain. First, Trumpism—as developed in collaboration with Trump's former advisor Steve Bannon—has proven to be far more multifaceted than UKIP's agenda. When initially crafted, it featured a protectionist trade agenda, a number of pro-labor perspectives, pro-Christian rhetoric, an isolationist foreign policy, and a virulently anti-immigrant, anti-Muslim approach that accompanied Trump's racist innuendo. Second, unlike with Brexit, the vast majority of Trump's most prominent policy promises have not been achieved yet. And one reason why is resistance from within the Republican Party.

### How will white working-class people change the Republican Party?

The allure of Trump and this hypothetical third party should be immediately important to the Republican Party: If Trump were the whole story and his message didn't matter, then Republicans could dismiss this election and presidency as an anomaly. However, Trump has clearly championed a policy agenda that has been latent in the Republican base, which will force the party to make a choice: adopt this agenda in the future or stick with its long-standing principles and risk alienating its other voters. That would either usher in a radical turn in the party's trajectory or open up space for a third party, the likes of which have grown rapidly in Europe.

It is worth acknowledging the reversal that much of Trumpism entails for the Republican establishment. For the last 50 years, the Republican Party has represented business interests. Even as the Democratic Party has made inroads with corporate America, it has attracted voters *despite* its economic policies, not because of them. Republicans have consistently pursued a program of significant tax cuts for the wealthy, whose businesses they have expanded with trade deals and shielded from accountability and the labor movement.

Republicans have been consistently against minimum-wage increases, new workplace standards, and trade protectionism. The Republican Party has also been characterized by interventionist foreign policy platforms, the advocates of which believe the United States has an obligation to lead the world and take an active role in the affairs of other nations that might affect American interests. For decades, moderate Republicans have argued for more open immigration policies that attract top talent to the United States and ensure a supply of low-skilled labor for businesses. Trump's stated ideas contradict nearly all of this.

This puts the Republican Party establishment in an un-enviable position. Based on my research, even had Trump lost in 2016, his movement of supporters would have likely yearned for others like him to fill the void in American politics. And if Republicans, in an attempt to appeal to Independent voters and the growing minority popula-tion, pivot away from Trump's rhetoric, they could face internal upheaval and perhaps even wide-scale defection to a third party. On the flip side, if Republicans do allow Trumpism to define the party, they risk ushering in an era of Democratic success. Hillary Clinton was the most divi-sive Democratic politician ever nominated for the White House. What if anyone other than she had run in 2016? What if Democrats made a more deliberate appeal to white working-class voters in order to keep those on the partisan margins? What if Trump disappoints a significant share of the Exasperated voters I discussed in Chapter 3?

Before Trump was elected, the conventional wisdom was that the Republican Party was near implosion. Whether authors were referring to the Republican Party's electoral chances or its historic ideals, the message was clear: Donald Trump has crafted a Republican Party that marginalizes the people who believed in its bedrock prin-ciples, and it narrowed its focus to a core of bitter white people who yearn for yesteryear. What few anticipated was the power of partisan ties and Hillary Clinton's inability to attract moderate Republicans and Independents.

If current voting trends hold, demographic change is in Democrats' favor. Urban and ethnic minority voters make up an increasing share of the American electorate, and white working-class people—subject to lower fertility rates, poorer health, and fewer resources—are shrinking. Republicans have overachieved thanks to sophisticated political strategy. They have extensively gerrymandered congressional districts in such a way that approximately 45 percent of all districts in the House of Representatives are Republican "safe" seats. They have benefited from the distortions provided by the Electoral university system. Since 1992, only one Republican presidential candidate has won a majority of the popular vote, and just barely: George W. Bush, with 50.7 percent of the vote in 2004. In these circumstances, for Republicans to maintain the white working-class vote-switchers that altered the electoral math in 2016, they will need to sustain at least some elements of Trumpism.

Most likely to survive any Washington compromises are Trump's outspoken views on immigration, race, and religion. After Trump's election, the political scientist John Sides undertook a thorough analysis of voting data that focused on the factors that were uniquely powerful in 2016 compared to 2012.[36] His research extends back to December 2011, so his findings do not reflect people who changed their attitudes to match their candidate preference—a common phenomenon in American politics.[37] The upshot is that, despite Trump's economic populism, the importance attached to entitlement programs, trade, and economic insecurity did not become more strongly associated with vote choice in 2016. These economic attitudes were found to be more consequences than causes of partisanship or vote choice. Instead, Sides found that the attitudes about immigration, feelings toward black people, and feelings toward Muslims became more strongly related to voting behavior in 2016.

Sides found that the increased salience of these attitudes was pivotal for Trump because a substantial number of Obama voters harbored less than favorable attitudes toward black people, Muslims, and immigrants:

- Thirty-seven percent of white Obama voters had a less than favorable attitude toward Muslims.
- Thirty-three percent of white Obama voters said that "illegal immigrants" were "mostly a drain," compared to 40 percent who said that they "mostly make a contribution."
- Thirty-four percent of white Obama voters said that it should be harder "for foreigners to immigrate to the United States," while just 33 percent said it should be easier and 21 percent said there should be no change.[38]

The salience of these attitudes related to immigration, race, and religion was not limited to white working-class people. Among white people with and without a university degree, attitudes toward both immigrants and Muslims had a stronger impact in 2016 than in 2012. However, there is evidence that racial attitudes were activated more among white people without a university degree than white people with a university degree. Economic anxiety was actually more prevalent among white people with a university degree.

Early in the Trump administration, the president and Republican Party acted accordingly. They employed sweeping executive actions to suspend United States' refugee admissions and enact a broader ban on people from multiple Muslim-majority countries. They beefed up immigration enforcement operations to detain and deport undocumented immigrants, including those without criminal records, and canceled the "Dreamer" program, Deferred Action for Childhood Arrivals (DACA). They ordered harsher sentencing for minor drug offenses, which predominantly affect young black males. They also canceled American participation in the Trans-Pacific Partnership trade agreement and the Paris Climate Change Agreement. Each of these acts symbolically appeals to the latent priorities of the Trump voter base, giving Republicans the license to pursue more traditional party prerogatives from Capitol Hill and in foreign policy.

This all projects a future Republican Party that employs "red meat" actions around immigration, race, and religion to satisfy the cultural prerogatives of white working-class people as it continues to pursue its usual fiscal agenda to satisfy the economic prerogatives of business interests. On the one hand, this seems to be a Frankenstein-like party, cobbled together to appeal to completely different constituencies that have been adversarial to one another historically. On the other hand, this strategy may be sustainable because it satisfies each constituency's principal priorities—much in the way the Democrats attempt to manage their unwieldy coalition. The real questions are whether business moderates will be turned off by the social division Republicans are instilling, and whether the salience of economic issues will eventually grow among more white working-class people, and whether the divisive boundaries between them and other working-class people remain.

### Do white working-class people vote against their own interests?

A common refrain among many frustrated people on the American and European Left is that white working-class people "vote against their own interests." Why, they ask, would the poor—who are so reliant on social programs and subsidies, who cannot afford health care, who are the beneficiaries of labor protections, who depend on public services—vote for political candidates and parties dedicated to dissolving these provisions to the benefit of the wealthy? Why would voters behave so irrationally?

A fundamental misunderstanding about white working-class interests is that these interests are singular and economic in nature. Many white working-class people balance a variety of interests at once. The average white working-class American or Briton likely supports a range of protectionist economic policies and a range of nativist social policies. Since the 1990s, no mainstream American or British party has advocated for protectionism in the way the Left once did. This shift has left greater contrasts in the realm of social policy. Where white working-class interests are singular, the data suggest that they care far more about social and cultural affairs than those pertaining to the economy. In other words, by supporting UKIP, Donald Trump, and Republicans, white working-class people do vote in their interests—their social interests, not their economic interests.

Observers who lament the irrationality of white working-class people who vote for right-wing parties rarely lament the irrationality of middle- and upper-income people who vote for left-wing parties. When middle- and upper-income people support the Left, they typically do so because they are willing to sacrifice their economic interests for their social interests. White working-class people effectively make a parallel sacrifice.

One of the primary conclusions of my research is that white working-class voters are absolutely rational. They seek representatives who care about their perspectives.

They seek platforms that act on these perspectives. And they respond to parties and organizations that invest in them with time, resources, and candidates. This is not different from any other group of voters. The difference is that social and economic forces have isolated the British and American white working class as a political constituency to the extent that many feel like an afterthought in the countries they once defined. They have responded with rebellion.

# 5

# PUBLIC DEBATES ABOUT WHITE WORKING-CLASS PEOPLE

*Was the white working class ever "on top"?*

Given their smaller numbers, diminished resources, and lack of political clout, the fact that white working-class people still feel a sense of status demonstrates that this status is more ideological than real. This ideology follows naturally from a culture that equates nativity with virtue. For the last 50 years, white working-class people in the United States and United Kingdom enjoyed a privileged place in the economy and society. Being white and native brought immense advantages: factories gave job openings to friends and family members, working men's clubs discriminated according to neighborhood, and government offices awarded housing and other benefits to citizens. Though idealized, these entitlements gave the white working class a sense of position, dignity, and centrality.

This feeling largely originated in the narratives that governments constructed to honor World War veterans in the 1920s and 1950s. Governments did this out of a sense of obligation and responsibility, but also in order to ensure that the public would remain committed to government causes after suffering such devastating losses. In the 1960s and 1970s, organized labor made similar appeals to their members—many of whom also served in World War II. Companies played along to build their image and keep workers committed to strenuous, backbreaking work.

More recently, white working-class centrality has been implied in efforts to assimilate immigrants. The United States, the United Kingdom, and Europe have encouraged immigrants to adopt national identities that are, presumably, already held by most white natives. Citizenship tests quiz immigrants on national history, traditions, norms, and institutions.[1] The American test has asked about the number of Supreme Court justices and the wars the United States has fought. The British test has asked about the population of Wales and what people eat for Christmas. These tests imply that a coherent national identity exists and is worth preserving, but critics have dismissed them as mere posturing. Looking at these tests reveals just how difficult it is to define a national identity. Despite a stated intention to promote a distinct national character, they tend to be so universal that they champion the principal tenets of a global liberal order, and ensure knowledge of trivia but little else.[2]

Beyond citizenship tests, these governments have paid mere lip service to the importance of native-born citizens in recent years. Instead, an elite-driven meritocracy promotes anyone who contributes value—regardless of their origin—but reinforces growing inequality for everyone else. This economy outsources production and recruits immigrants to do the skilled jobs that locals can't do and the unskilled jobs that locals won't do. Working-class white people get the message: they are replaceable.

The sense that white working-class people were once "on top" stems from the greater economic opportunities that people without university degrees once had and the privileged status white people once held. It ignores the history of intense labor struggles, political dependency, dangerous jobs, cultural division, and economic precariousness that has always defined the white working-class experience.

White working-class labor was often dangerous and poorly paid.[3] Struggles to improve working conditions and wages were tumultuous, pitting workers against their employers. Mechanization divided skilled from unskilled workers as greater skill brought the advantages of more income, stability, and social prestige.[4] In the workplace, employers used dehumanizing strategies to manage the masses. Steel workers, for example, were identified by accounting numbers and required to display these numbers on badges they wore while on the job.[5] Workers did circumvent and resist. Laborers often resorted to disobedience, sabotage, and theft to challenge management.[6] Yet the workplace reshaped workers' identities in often crude and alienating ways.[7]

Beyond the workplace, white working-class individuals were condescended to by the middle and upper classes. In the United Kingdom, dress, appearance, mannerisms, and speech determined one's job prospects.[8] In America, the white working class was policed by Protestant ideals, encouraged to forgo laziness, backwardness, and rudeness for the gentility of middle-class standards.[9] White working-class status was what one ought to rapidly leave behind.[10]

Joining the American middle class was difficult and uncertain, particularly for women. For working-class women, the move to the suburbs could often feel like a "crisis" as they became isolated and lost traditional social supports.[11] Women had to further contend with the overwhelming patriarchy of the working-class household: expectations kept them away from paid work despite their families' limited budgets, and domestic violence had few, if any, remedies.[12] Some workers abandoned the goal of home ownership to focus on their children's possible success.[13] More prosperous white working-class families approached home ownership as a means of attaining the full American Dream.[14] It decreased dependence on wages and cash assets, creating some sense of autonomy.[15]

Yet suburbia was itself a middle- and upper-class concept, and a way to quell the working class's discontent, brought on by a lack of political independence.[16] Powerful families controlled how workers could work and relax. In the steel towns, companies sponsored everything from bowling tournaments to amusement parks.[17] Companies relied on a mix of physical intimidation and dependency-creating incentives (including subsidized home loans, bonuses, stock options, and insurance) to secure workers' loyalty.[18] They recruited public police forces, encouraged espionage, and stockpiled weapons against strikers.[19] They leveraged racial divisions to undermine worker solidarity on the job and in the segregated neighborhoods and dormitories they controlled.[20] Companies swayed local politics, contributing to political campaigns, taxes, land purchases, services, and community payrolls outright.[21] They also covertly created company-dominated unions or so-called Employee Representation Plans to hurt independent unions.[22] Workers' hard-earned unions, however, soon became bureaucracies in their own right, making concessions in the name of stable wages and consistent employment.[23] The ability of the rank and file to strike for change was curtailed by an overwhelming reliance on formalized collective bargaining.[24] In time, even local unions would find fault with their national counterparts as successive management demands were met with conciliatory "bargains."[25]

Rapid industrial decline took away not only jobs but also the means by which white working-class individuals contributed to the nation. Employment allowed white working-class individuals to literally build America.[26]

Work justified white working-class citizenship. Now, these contributions are a source of conflicting, if not debilitating, nostalgia.

The postapocalyptic feel of many white working-class communities demonstrates a loss of *defining* resources. It's not that white working-class individuals were once "on top," but that they once had relatively stable, working-class lives (if not a road to the middle class). Today, the white working class struggles to maintain the traditions that once defined their workplaces, neighborhoods, and bars *without* the same resources. Rather than attempting to achieve an advanced social status, white working-class individuals are now struggling to keep hold of what defines their lower status. But the dream of mobility continues to hold sway, despite glaring inconsistencies.

This fall is also reflected in media representations of the white working class. The alternative household of *Modern Family* has taken over Archie Bunker's living room in *All in the Family*. And where working-class drama persists, white working-class men are overshadowed by white women and working-class people of color.[27] Among the reality TV shows and boxing biopics that continue to depict white working-class masculinities, protagonists are validated only insofar as they remain "respectable" or entertain a middle- and upper-class fascination with the working-class hero.[28] Pushed out of textbooks and sidelined in popular entertainment, white working-class narratives are marked as problematic or abnormal in their totalizing whiteness.[29] Increasingly, white working-class individuals are marked as "anachronistic."[30]

These changing representations reflect real changes on the ground. Many white working-class neighborhoods are now highly diverse. White working-class people feel left behind by well-off whites, competitive with minority neighbors, and vilified by urban cosmopolitans.

The increasingly critical discussion of white privilege intensifies this perceived persecution.[31] And unlike other minority constituencies, white working-class individuals have had difficulty articulating their losses. Under these circumstances, the past looks downright rosy.

### Are white working-class people "trapped" in poverty?

White working-class people are trapped in poverty, but no more than other groups.[32] Like the children of ethnic minorities, children in white working-class families often have little to inherit other than a struggle with persistent poverty. They are poorly protected from abrupt economic changes or unanticipated accidents.[33] They face worse health outcomes.[34] They lack wealth. Their income is lower. The property values of their homes are often precarious, and they generally lack cash assets.[35] Increasingly, there is no safety net.

White working-class individuals are poorer than their middle- and upper-class fellows. In the United States, white working-class men lag behind national averages on several fronts. By the end of 2016, the unemployment rate among white working-class men was 6.4 percent compared to a national figure of 4.7 percent. While overall labor-force participation among men fell from 87 percent in 1948 to 69 percent in 2017, labor-force participation among white working-class men has declined further to 59 percent. Although average hourly wages have increased by 2.9 percent a year, the hourly wages of white working-class men have increased only by 2.8 percent a year—a small difference that, when compounded over 27 years, accounts for an ever-widening gap between relative wages.[36] Given these obstacles, many white working-class individuals have forsaken formal work altogether only to participate in an equally unstable, informal economy.

What are white working-class individuals' chances of moving up the economic ladder? Not good. The United States is now one of the world's most unequal societies.[37] An American child born in the bottom quintile of the income distribution has only a 7.5 percent chance of reaching the top quintile. Canadian children are about two times more likely than American children to realize the "American Dream."[38] In the United Kingdom, high inequality similarly stunts upward income mobility.[39]

Mobility in the United States also varies widely across regions. Some areas display upward mobility rates akin to those of highly mobile Northern European countries. Others have the lowest rates of upward mobility ever recorded. In regions with the highest rates of mobility, children have greater than a 16 percent chance of moving from the bottom fifth to the top fifth of the income distribution. In areas with the lowest rates of mobility, children have less than a 5 percent chance.[40] Urban areas are typically worse off than rural ones, but the rural children who advance often move away to pursue employment elsewhere.[41] Areas with greater racial and income segregation, more urban sprawl, high income inequality, low school quality, low social capital, and more single mothers typically display lower rates of upward income mobility.[42] Many of these factors impact an individual's youth, suggesting that the disadvantages of a worse-off environment shape life prospects *during* childhood.[43]

Differences in university attendance and potential earnings between children born in the bottom and top quintiles have also remained steady since the 1970s. Modern jobs often require a university education, at minimum. But white working-class children are not going to university at the same rates as their peers, and those who are well beyond their university years have few means of gaining the skills required to enter a transformed job market. Between 1996 and 2014, white men who completed a university education saw their wages and salary income increase by 133 percent in the first 20 years of their careers. White men with only a high school education witnessed a mere 19 percent increase during this interval.[44]

Consequently, older white working-class individuals are increasingly isolated. They find themselves falling behind as the requirements for higher-paying jobs become more and more rigorous. The achievement gap between younger children of low-income and high-income families is also widening.[45] Schools have been accused of reproducing the "relations of domination and subordination necessary to the maintenance of a capitalist economy."[46] Increasingly, the white working class of tomorrow will be the descendants of white working-class families today.

On the job, there is less demand, lower pay, and fewer apprenticeships for unskilled manual workers. Working-class employment takes place in call centers, warehouses, restaurants, hotels, or behind the wheel of a vehicle. Transient employment substantially curtails opportunities to form new social networks around work. The stigmatization of temporary work often leads temporary workers to dissociate from one another.[47] As social networks continue to shrink, white working-class individuals have relatively few resources to prepare for the turbulence of the new economy. They are frequently disoriented by the middle-class behaviors and habits they are encouraged to adopt at work.[48]

Disadvantaged communities, many of them in post-traumatic cities, fared poorly during both the Great Recession and during the period of general economic recovery.[49] One study assessed 25,000 zip codes across the United States using the distressed communities index—a combined measure of economic well-being factoring in the number of adults without high school diplomas, poverty rates, prevalence of vacant houses, number of unemployed adults, average incomes, business stability, and job opportunities.[50] Many of the most distressed communities were within the Rust Belt.[51] Differences between the most distressed 10 percent of postal codes and most prosperous 10 percent were sizable; for instance, the most distressed American zip codes had a median income at 63 percent of their state's average while the most prosperous had a median income at 158 percent of their state's average.[52] These differences likely contributed to an unequal recovery following the Great Recession. Distressed communities witnessed a 6.7 percent *decline* in employment during the recovery while prosperous communities benefited from a 17.4 percent *increase* in employment.[53]

Movement from a low-mobility city to a high-mobility city can offset the negative effects of living in communities with little support. A child's adult income earnings are proportionally raised by the amount of time he or she lives in the better-off location.[54] But many white working-class individuals currently living in low-mobility places lack the financial resources to move elsewhere. The white working class is "trapped in poverty." With low intergenerational mobility and increasing income inequality in the United States and United Kingdom, a child born into a white working-class family has little chance of making it big, or making it at all.

### How has the decline in unions affected white working-class politics?

At peak membership, unions allowed the white working class to engage with the political system and bargain for change. As recently as 1983, the share of American workers in unions was 20.1 percent. Even in 1995, 32.4 percent of British private-sector workers were unionized. However, industrial collapse and changes in labor laws

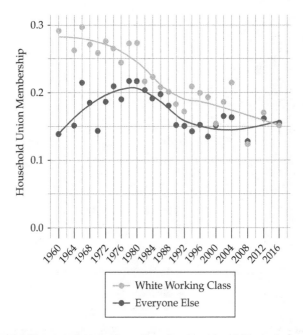

**Figure 5.1** The proportion of white working-class American adults who live in a household with at least one union member, 1960–2016.

*Source:* American National Election Studies cumulative file.

drove significant de-unionization.[55] In 2016, 10.7 percent of American workers were unionized.[56] And by 2013, only 14.4 percent of British private-sector workers were unionized.[57] Figures 5.1 and 5.2 exhibit the precipitous drop in membership specifically among white working-class people in the United States and United Kingdom. While de-unionization clearly weakened the political organization and power of white working-class people, the absence of unions also stopped many from finding new roads for advocacy. In this way, the decline of unions produced a "hangover" effect.

On the surface, unions seemed to be democratic bastions of working-class politics. They represented the

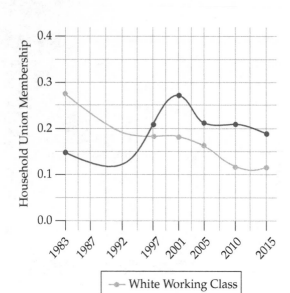

**Figure 5.2** The proportion of white working-class British adults who belong to a labor union, 1983–2015. The increase among "everyone else" is likely attributable to public-sector union membership.

*Source*: British Election Study.

primary connection between white workers and politics. Unions arbitrated local disputes between workers and their employers. They provided the physical space for white workers' political activities on a larger scale. Among white working-class individuals, unions were a source of social capital. They placed working-class compatriots in direct contact with one another, fostering a sense of shared fate and responsibility. They represented workers in negotiations with industry and in the public, helping crystallize class formation and awareness of working-class concerns.[58] Unions were the places politicians would visit to solicit white working-class votes.[59]

Although unions began with self-ownership and self-governance,[60] their leaders eventually resorted to corrupt practices, including voter fraud and assassination.[61] Unions also discriminated in their membership and in leadership selection—mimicking the double standards of race that companies applied on factory floors. Union leadership also grew distant and more autocratic in their dealings with the working people they ostensibly represented.[62] With industrial decline, leadership minimized workers' demands, compromising with employers in the name of continued productivity, secure wages, and stable job opportunities. In this manner, unions reproduced company power, and in their time of great need, workers could not rely on union bailouts. This muddling of corporate and worker interests would continue to impact collective bargaining outcomes well past the prime of industry. Union collusion with companies in the 1980s, for instance, left workers with few options as their hours shrank, jobs disappeared, benefits decreased, and wages fell.

Worse, rather than create networks that could outlast themselves, unions created institutional dependency. Unions not only handled collective bargaining on behalf of workers, but also offered their members a space to advocate. The process of advocacy was frequently left up to a nonconsultative labor bureaucracy.[63] The practice of grievance resolution among unions, for example, funneled worker discontent through a long chain of bureaucratic steps that distanced workers from any resolution; representatives replaced workers as the primary actors for workplace reform.[64] Company unions, introduced before World War I, were effectively used as a means to control worker self-initiative.[65] They replaced "working-class solidarity" with "company solidarity."[66] Workers would "aid management" rather than act independently for their own interests.[67] By the middle of the twentieth century, while some workers undertook wildcat strikes, many were lulled into the complacency of waiting for the union to act for them or tell them when to act. Others were lost when the space for activism disappeared with their job.

Unions featured a strictly top-down hierarchical structure. This discouraged any rank-and-file initiative and promoted closed channels of communication networks at the top that relied on backroom deals.[68] Consequently, memberships became ill-informed and passive—a unionism that reacted to employer initiatives, rather than move proactively.[69] Unions fought radicalism and contained internal opposition, such that the rank and file did not realize their clout independent of unions.[70] The rigid structure and concentration of power further prevented many workers from ever taking on substantive leadership roles.[71]

While this consolidated unions' power during their heyday, this power disappeared with unions during their decline. As local economies lost their largest employers, social structures crumbled. While new corporate giants in fast food, retail, and the service sectors have filled in, many of them tend to have loosely connected branches and franchises that foster little collectivism among their employees. Further, such jobs typically do not position employees in circumstances that require a great deal of interdependency and teamwork. Flexible labor supplies lead to high turnover, and the computerization of basic tasks reduces the importance of bonding with fellow employees.

After the collapse of unions, white working-class people have failed to find a consistent, alternative outlet. The drop in union clout led traditional leftist parties to reduce union engagement and ignore white working-class marginalization in order to appeal to diversifying electorates. As a consequence, avenues for meaningful political engagement have narrowed, leaving some white working-class individuals vulnerable to the Radical Right. Perhaps more alarmingly, others have grown entirely apathetic toward politics.

As unions deteriorated, the racial divisions they previously encouraged also hindered the formation of independent, substantive ties between workers.[72] This discord accelerated the decline in membership and helped estrange the white working class from unions.

Increasingly, unions have welcomed women and minorities. In 2016, black workers in the United States were more likely to be union members than white workers, and the gap between union membership rates of men and women was significantly narrower than in 1983.[73] Unions are no longer the predominant domain of white male workers. They are familiar places turned unfamiliar and, consequently, no longer predictably deliver white working-class votes.

Other traditional sites of working-class politics have also suffered under deindustrialization. Pubs and blue-collar taverns, for example, are increasingly scarce.[74] These establishments were more than social spots after work.[75] In many cases, they were key spaces for mass meetings and grassroots mobilizing. Labor organizers, for example, first met at a local tavern ahead of what would become a major Chicago strike in 1937.[76] While internet-organized petitions, demonstrations, boycotts, and blogging offer novel means of political activism, they are less accessible to those without reliable internet access or time. Lacking faith in institutions, many white working-class people have decided to take matters into their own hands. The 2011 London riots, for instance, expressed a sense of frustration through violence, but few participants acknowledged a unity of purpose. Since de-unionization, white working-class individuals have simply struggled to define themselves, convey their collective concerns, and effectively lobby political leaders.

### What does the left have to do to win working-class white votes?

Fewer left-wing politicians and parties win white working-class votes.[77] Over the last 30 years, there has been an exodus of white working-class people from the ideological and partisan Left. In order to better understand how prominent Leftists can win this constituency, I visited Democratic Governor Steve Bullock in Montana. While Hillary Clinton lost Montana by more than 23 points in the 2016 presidential election, Bullock was narrowly reelected, winning by a margin of 50 to 46 percent. In his predominantly white working-class state, Democrats have won four straight gubernatorial races and maintained one US Senate seat since 1913. Do Montana Democrats have a template that can be applied elsewhere? What does Steve Bullock know that Hillary Clinton's army of consultants and advisors missed? Indeed, how can local politics inform a more national strategy for general elections and down-ballot races?

I started in Great Falls, Montana. A gritty, working-class town on the banks of the Missouri River, it is a post-traumatic city. An industrial hub, Great Falls used to be anchored by the Anaconda Company—once America's fourth largest corporation—which provided a third of Montana's paychecks from its railroad, logging, mining, and refining operations. In the years since, Great Falls's manufacturing sector has shrunk and its unions have been undercut; the surrounding landscape of ranchers now supplies an international market for meat and grain, and a once reliably Democratic region is far more contested by Republicans and frustrated by the status quo. In interviews with locals, I found exhaustion with detached national Democrats, and a pervasive appreciation of straight talk. Trump voters who also supported Governor Bullock abound.

What makes Governor Bullock such an interesting case study for the Democratic Party is that he isn't exactly a unicorn—that rare, transcendent candidate whose personality crosses social divides. He simply combines a reassuring cultural style with a practical progressive message on issues that people care about. That recipe seems to work for more than one personality type. The rather unassuming Bullock was preceded by the charismatic and bombastic Brian Schweitzer, a Democratic governor whose plain-spoken swagger appealed to Montanans and frustrated his rivals. Schweitzer famously wielded branding irons to publicly veto bills passed by a Republican-controlled legislature.

"I do best at explaining things by telling a story," Schweitzer told me. "Young people approach me who want to go into politics, and they ask me what to do. I would change your major out of political science or law. Get a practical trade, study science or math. Go out and try to change the world in the private sector. Start a business and lose it. Start a family. . . . Do not learn how to run this country by working for people who already do. Look at congressional staffers. In twenty years, they'll all be in office themselves—looking, talking, and droning on like the ones we have right now."

Schweitzer wasn't referring to Bullock, but the governor could be forgiven for thinking so. Were he in Washington, Bullock would fit right in. Though gregarious, he is also cerebral, measured, even wonkish. After law school, he worked as a legal counsel to the Montana secretary of state, and he was later promoted to executive assistant attorney general and chief deputy attorney general before being elected Montana's attorney general in 2008.

I asked Bullock if Schweitzer, whose name had been mentioned in 2020 presidential chatter, offered any memorable pieces of guidance before he was term-limited in 2012. "We lead in different ways," he said. However, it is Bullock's way that Democrats are more capable of reproducing elsewhere. Without being that once-in-a-generation politician, he is able to connect with rural and working-class white voters with symbolic messaging and a platform that keeps them in mind.

When I was in Great Falls, Bullock came to the A. T. Klemens metal shop to promote a new bill that would give tax credits to businesses that hired apprentices and veterans. He would later tour the workshop machinery and observe the craft of several young apprentices. It was all a bit forced, but what Bullock lacked in magnetism, he compensated for with his propensity to honor the past before pursuing the future. He looked at a small room of metalworkers and said, "We look on the horizon and we think that's what's going to limit our growth is a shortage of guys like this. But that extends to other sectors like IT too." Bullock was celebrating both Montana's past and its future—and honoring people who work with their hands.

White working-class people are accustomed to being considered anachronisms with no place in America's high-tech, information economy. Donald Trump was the first presidential candidate in a generation to make a deliberate appeal to this constituency and envision an economy that valued their contribution. Hillary Clinton was the establishment candidate, but also one who heralded and symbolized a future that reoriented the country's workplace, society, and relationship with a globalized world. The election was a referendum on America's past.

"Steve's been able to honor industries of the past," said Nancy Keenan, the chairwoman of the Montana Democratic Party. "Timber, mining, coal. He has said that's part of who we are, but also talk about how do we grow and what the future looks like. He has been able to keep a foot in each of those worlds. He just recognizes economically a changing world. The days of mining—I grew up in a mining town, it's all we knew—you'll still have them as part of Montana's economy but it'll change because of technology and a global marketplace. It goes back to trust. They trust him, and trust that he has their best interests at heart."

Bullock has earned that trust by first identifying with Montanans. That has lent him the credibility to veto more bills than any Montana governor in history and also pass progressive bills without alienating too many social conservatives. He has voted against broadening access to guns, enrolled Montana in Obamacare, pushed for universal preschool, introduced new funding for infrastructure, and, while I was in town, received an award from Planned Parenthood. Meanwhile, bills like the apprenticeship tax incentive serve Montanans without university educations and veterans, and they keep business owners happy. Bullock eases his constituents into a progressive future by weaning them off the past instead of insisting on a sharp break.

Policy platforms aside, Keenan insisted that her candidates can't win statewide office in Montana without "a story." What is Steve Bullock's? "I think Steve does connect with white working-class voters," she said. "With his knowledge of Montana. He grew up here. He hunts and he fishes."

I asked the same question to Dave Hunter, a Montana Democratic political strategist since 1978. "White working-class men like to hunt, and they like to fish," he said. "Fifty percent of Montana residents have a fishing license; 20 percent have a hunting license, and Bullock does too." Even Andrew Bardwell, a 40-year-old bison rancher whom I met in a farm store, said, "Bullock represents average Montanans. He hunts, he fishes, he's a businessman." "The irony is that I don't think he does [like to hunt and fish],"

Hunter confessed. "Yeah he's hunted, but not for awhile. But it is the cultural messaging." He thought for a moment. "I mean, he can produce pictures of him and his buddies hunting," he continued. "They put them up on Facebook, but I haven't seen one for four years. There's both a cultural test that is ethnocentric, and then you need an economic message. If you really are one of us, then people will listen to the economic message. If you're not really one of us, then nothing else matters."

Bullock's campaign exploited this ethnocentrism by drawing attention to his 2016 Republican opponent Greg Gianforte's roots in New Jersey and California. (He would later win Montana's sole congressional seat, despite assaulting a news reporter just before the election.)

Every successful statewide Montana Democrat has been able to sell himself as an average, local man—and they all have been local men—even when there is countervailing evidence about how average they are. Not only do they revere the region's heritage but they embed themselves in it. Montana's former at-large congressman, Pat Williams, served in the House of Representatives for 18 years and consistently made references to his jobs as a miner, sewer serviceman, and track layer for the Butte-Anaconda-Pacific railroad hauling ore to smelters. Never mind that he held all those jobs before he graduated from university.

Max Baucus, a longtime US senator, came from one of Montana's wealthiest families, but he is known as a rancher from north of Helena who once walked 800 miles across Montana while campaigning. Jon Tester, a current senator, actively farms 1,800 acres northeast of Great Falls and is prone to poking fun at city folk.

"It's authenticity," Keenan said. "Candidates have to be true to themselves. People want you to be authentic, to share their experiences. When grain prices fall through the floor and the entire community is feeling the pinch,

Montanans want you to understand that. You don't have to always agree with them, but you do need to look them in the eye and be honest with them. John Tester says, 'Don't tell me something's not happening with the climate; my crops are harvesting three weeks ahead.' His hands are in the dirt. The Democratic Party is full of these damned do-gooders. A lot of the people who run as Democrats think that if we could just get into the depths and detail of the policy and make people understand it, then we'll get elected. Oh, hell no! The detail doesn't matter, people! What's the first rule of politics? Show up. Everywhere. The second rule is: Show up where they didn't want or ask you to come. I used to show up at the stock growers convention or the Chamber of Commerce conventions, and they'd all ask, 'What the hell is she doing here?'" She guffawed. "And I'd tell everyone how terrific it was to be with them."

In an eerie echo, when I asked Governor Bullock what national Democrats need to do, he said, "They need to recognize that there are no such things as national issues; they're all local. It's not about pigeonholing issues to score votes. Rule number one is to show up, and if you're just going to write off parts of the country, your success will be limited. I think that we need to have a 50-state strategy. In 2008, you'd be tripping over Obama people [in Montana]. President Obama brought his wife and kids to the Butte Fourth of July Parade. They lost Montana by 2 points, and he came after the primary."

In an era when so much of politics is mediated by cable news, scripted social media missives, and airbrushed web profiles, showing up reveals candidates' humanity. It is where bonds are born.

But can nostalgic stories create bonds in coastal Americans? What bonds can emerge when the candidate who shows up is a shotgun-toting, coal-dusted, grain-farming moderate?

Perhaps the Democratic Party is simply too unwieldy a co-alition. The Women's March on January 21, 2017, revealed a very heterogeneous leftist coalition. Can such an eclectic community expand to include the voices of marginalized white working-class people from postindustrial spaces?

"You can't," Dave Hunter said. "There is a disconnect between the things a Democratic candidate has to do to win primaries in California and New York, and what is culturally acceptable for white persuadable voters in Montana. Look at Tester and Baucus, they are always running away from the national party. They pitch them-selves as an independent voice for Montana. There isn't any national messaging. Running on a national party platform is death. In a state that is almost exclusively white, the imagery of the national Democratic Party as a multicultural, liberal, gun-control, anticoal party is tough messaging."

"Yeah, I suppose it's a benefit, the homogeneity," Bullock told me, upon reflection. "But if the premise is that Democrats have lost white working-class men, then that could be a [national] problem, yeah. In 2020, you could weave together a coalition based on identity politics. If that's the bedrock foundation, you might win the presi-dency, but you'll lose the country. I don't want to be part of a party that ideologically only reflects the East and West Coasts. And while our experiences are different, I think a Native American, Latino, or me, as parents, have the same aspirations for our kids. Your hopes are the same."

However, many Democrats believe that broadening their party further only thins the glue that holds them to-gether. Recent research by Matt Grossmann and David A. Hopkins shows that Democrats are a coalition of di-verse identity groups—African Americans, Latinos, youth, and women—to whom the party directly sells its policies.[78] Yet this has left little space for other interests.

Currently, searching for rural Democrats in the national party caucus is, as they say in Montana, "diggin' where there ain't no taters." There is little space for Montana's former congressman Pat Williams, who was broadly against gun control; its former governor, Brian Schweitzer, who supported the construction of oil pipelines; or Senator Jon Tester, who pushed for the once-endangered gray wolf to be fair hunting game. In turn, the party of diversity appears inhospitable for such a group of working-class voters of Montana. The Montana experience suggests that Democrats must either compromise or risk being ideologically "pure," but confined to their strongholds in coastal cities.

What is so frustrating to older leftists is that Donald Trump resurrected the David versus Goliath themes that once characterized the Democratic identity of yesteryear. Certainly, Democrats still support the wage standards, infrastructure, and redistributive policy prescriptions they once touted and that have since been mimicked by President Trump. Why are these principles no longer credible to enough working-class people—regardless of whether they are white? When I posed this question to political strategists who have worked extensively in Montana, the consensus is that progressive platforms cannot be proposed without the cultural symbolism that "shows" rather than "tells" the white working class that they matter, that they belong.

Much of what I took away from my research in Montana emphasized the importance of style, of rhetoric, of going local, connecting with constituents and "showing up." The substance of Democratic—and Labour—Party issues is not drastically different from Montana to Massachusetts, from Manchester to Middleborough. But style is variable. Politics is ultimately about symbolism, performance, and personality. White working-class people see their status as ideological in nature. As cheap as it is for politicians to honor that status and the heritage that underpins it, Democrats and Labour leaders have done little to do so. In many cases, this is out of fear of offending their ascendant base of ethnic minorities. However, it also stems from the fact that these parties have grown distant from white working-class constituencies—and show little desire to reach or reincorporate them. What party with national ambitions can afford to ignore or jettison such an enormous group of voters?

To renew their bond, the Left must demonstrate genuine interest and empathy; they must make a deliberate appeal for support. Such identity politics requires neither racism nor favoritism; it requires the extension of dignity. Democratic and Labour officials regularly cite the grievances of Muslims in the same sentence as they acknowledge the experiences of black people. They regularly make special trips to Latino neighborhoods and speak in Spanish if able. Doing so dignifies these communities by incorporating them into the discussion, by making their plight worthy of consideration. The Radical Right has dignified white working-class communities and grievances by making symbolic appeals to the ideas of heritage and sacrifice—something that should be equally available to the Left, sans the implicit xenophobia and racist undertones. Were the Left to make such symbolic appeals and targeted visits, it would get them an audience for their policy agenda.

However, to suggest that the appeal to white working-class people is a matter of style diminishes the extent to which the Left has compromised its substantive support for pro-working-class policies over the last 30 years. In the late 1980s, the Democratic Leadership Council aligned the party with the financial class. New Labor followed suit in Britain in the mid-1990s. Both parties' appeals to liberal, urban cosmopolitans and professionals complicated their relationship with unions and working people who supported far more protectionist positions. And as Democrats and Laborites have further embraced free trade, immigration, and multinational corporations, the economic policy distinctions between Left and Right became murkier, and white working-class people found less and less to like. The Left must identify new ways to embrace the realities and opportunities of globalization, but push policies that protect people from its excesses—new ways to make globalization freer, fairer, and more profitable for all.

The research by John Sides is daunting. It suggests that the driving force of white working-class Americans' attraction to Donald Trump was anti-immigrant sentiment and racial resentment—not the *economic* anxieties, but the *cultural* anxieties, created by globalization. Those cultural anxieties triumphed because there was no compelling Democratic alternative. Hillary Clinton effectively redlined white working-class people both rhetorically in her "deplorables" label and strategically in her absence from white working-class constituencies. A substantial number of white working-class people previously supported Democrats, despite the party's unabashed support for civil rights and more liberal immigration policies. This segment of white working-class people simply needs a reason to listen again.

### Can white working-class problems be solved?

The inclination to jettison white working-class people is strategically ill-advised, but also against our human impulses. Perhaps the most prominent expression of this unfortunate inclination is in the saying "demography is destiny." Recited widely first by Democrats in Washington and subsequently by some Labourites in Westminster, this refrain is derived from the projections that white— and particularly white working class—people comprise a dwindling share of the electorate, and eventually the co-alition of urban cosmopolitans and ethnic minorities will outnumber them. Such a simplistic philosophy assumes that political coalitions do not change over time with the nature of new public challenges. Worse, the hubristic im-plication is that the Left can be complacent; their ultimate victory is imminent and unconditional on their evolution with people's changing attitudes.

The "demography is destiny" slogan is also a way to justify the vilification and dismissal of white working-class people. It suggests that white working-class people's "racism," "welfare dependency," "addiction," and "family anarchy" warrant their dismissal.[79] This supposedly looming extinction lends reason to the Left's incremental abandonment of many rural and postindustrial districts. And this validates the lack of action to address severe so-cial problems and help white working-class communities retake control over their futures. "Demography is des-tiny" comforts policymakers into inaction in the face of intimidating challenges for governance: What can public policy do to revive the economic prospects of a 48-year-old parent of three children without any employable skills? What can government planning do to turn around the fortunes of a postapocalyptic steel town? What can lead-ership do to mollify the concerns about immigrants in an aging rural town that interacts with no foreigners? What should be done to help communities on the path to death?

To extend this metaphor, the humanitarian response to a person's pending death is hospice care—the provi-sion of comfort and treatment to mercifully relieve any pain, and permit their families to live. Donald Trump and the Radical Right have provided white working-class people with comfort in dignifying their feelings and circumstances. But their hollow promises to turn back the clock, reopen shuttered mills, reverse globalization, and invert demographic change represent an opiate. They whisper to white working-class people what they want to hear in the short term, but do little to assure that their families may live and thrive in a more prosperous future. Slowly, there is growing political capital behind real ideas to strengthen the social safety net, subsidize training and apprenticeships, and ease the burden of student loans. But these ideas are stopgaps. They are easing the pressure, rather than resolving the problem. How can we create avenues for people born into these communities to live vibrant and dynamic lives of possibility?

We can start both by creating more accessible avenues to education and training and by ensuring that the quality of available education and training is not contingent on an individual's wealth. White working-class people are who they are because of their level of educational attainment—economically, yes, but also by definition. Advanced and wider access to education is what has made the global economy and unmade those who have not adapted. More than ever before, education is the avenue to intergenerational mobility—the fundamental truth at the core of the meritocracy the world is striving to create. It will be what allows a steel town to raise children who are not predestined for manufacturing, but also what integrates the marginalized into a more global society. And yet poor communities have poor schools. And rich communities have rich schools that prepare their children for the emerging world to come. This reinforces the death of dying communities. Our system of education is not allowing us to create a break, an intervention, where we actually help these communities destined for death to revive.

Any revival, however, will take place in an alternative social and demographic environment. Thanks to immigration, differential fertility rates, and increasing numbers of people with university degrees, white working-class people's numbers and power will continue to dwindle. They are best served by bonding with other minority groups to secure a better future for disadvantaged people on society's margins. Right now, the white working-class minority and working-class ethnic minorities are prone to unproductive arguments about "who has it worse"—a debate that yields no winners. Their prospects for revival will be raised when they recognize that debt, inaccessible health care, addiction, poor schools, and inequality are scourges that respect no ethnic or racial boundaries. Their prospects for revival depend on the redefinition of white working-class politics into an inclusive politics of the working class more broadly.

Revivals—from music to literature—tend to rely on the work of the past, updating it, challenging it. However, the nostalgia of current political appeals to white working-class people reveres the past uncritically, paralyzing the evolution of their communities. And so it has entailed attempts to reinstate the pre-traumatic past, rather than adapt to the post-traumatic future. If it is to be successful, this revival requires a realignment of politics for a global world where parties are not advocating for Left or Right, but Open or Closed. It requires a realignment of policy to ensure that, as technology and industry advance faster than public institutions, people are not left behind. Ultimately, this revival requires us to question the status quo and some of its most sacred features: the power of entrenched social hierarchies, the status assigned to national heritage, and the reality of equal opportunity for all.

# NOTES

**Chapter 1**

1. David R. Roediger, *The Wages of Whiteness: Race and the Making of the American Working Class* (London: Verso, 1991).
2. Ibid.
3. Michael Omi and Howard Winant, *Racial Formation in the United States*, 3rd ed. (New York: Routledge, 2014).
4. Nell Irving Painter, *The History of White People* (New York: W. W. Norton, 2011).
5. Ibid.
6. W. E. B. Du Bois, *Black Reconstruction in America* (New York: Harcourt, Brace and Co., 1935).
7. Edmund S. Morgan, *American Slavery, American Freedom: The Ordeal of Colonial Virginia* (New York: W. W. Norton, 1975), p. 319.
8. As quoted in Michael Collins, *The Likes of Us: A Biography of the White Working Class* (London: Granta, 2004), p. 17.
9. Rogers M. Smith, *Civic Ideals: Conflicting Visions of Citizenship in US History* (New Haven, CT: Yale University Press, 1999).
10. Ian Haney López, *White by Law: The Legal Construction of Race* (New York: New York University Press, 1996).
11. Noel Ignatiev, *How the Irish Became White* (New York: Routledge, 1995).
12. Richard Dyer, *White: Essays on Race and Culture* (New York: Routledge, 1997), p. 1.

13. Karen Brodkin, "How Did Jews Become White Folks?,"
    in *Race*, edited by Steven Gregory and Roger Sanjek (New
    Brunswick, NJ: Rutgers University Press, 1994), pp. 78–99,
    86–89; Ignatiev, *How the Irish Became White*, p. 96; Roediger,
    *The Wages of Whiteness*, pp. 133–137; Rudolph Vecoli, "Are
    Italian Americans Just White Folks?" *Italian Americana* 13,
    no. 2 (1995): pp. 149–161; Theodore P. Wright, "The Identity
    and Changing Status of Former Elite Minorities: The
    Contrasting Cases of North Indian Muslims and
    American WASPs," in *Rethinking Ethnicity: Majority Groups
    and Dominant Minorities*, edited by Eric P. Kaufmann
    (New York: Routledge), pp. 31–38; Oren Yiftachel,
    "'Ethnocracy' and Its Discontents: Minorities, Protest and the
    Israeli Polity," *Critical Inquiry* 26 (2000): pp. 725–756.
14. Eric P. Kaufmann, email to author, July 23, 2014.
15. Collins, *The Likes of Us*, p. 263.
16. Eric P. Kaufmann, *The Rise and Fall of Anglo-America*
    (Cambridge, MA: Harvard University Press, 2004), p. 19.
17. Alan Abramowitz and Ruy Teixeira, "The Decline of
    the White Working Class and the Rise of a Mass Upper
    Middle Class," *Political Science Quarterly* 124, no. 3
    (2009): pp. 391–422.
18. See Stanley Aronowitz, *How Class Works: Power and Social
    Movement* (New Haven, CT: Yale University Press, 2003), p. 3.
19. See Robert MacDonald, "Labours of Love: Voluntary Working
    in a Depressed Local Economy," *Journal of Social Policy* 25,
    no. 1 (1996): pp. 19–38; Robert MacDonald, "Fiddly Jobs,
    Undeclared Working and the Something for Nothing Society,"
    *Work, Employment and Society* 8, no. 4 (1994): pp. 507–530.
20. See Abramowitz and Teixeira, "The Decline of the White
    Working Class"; Michèle Lamont, *The Dignity of Working
    Men: Morality and the Boundaries of Race, Class, and Immigration*
    (New York: Russell Sage Foundation, 2000), p. 2.
21. Abramowitz and Teixeira, "The Decline of the White Working
    Class."

22. See Tony Bennett et al., *Culture, Class, Distinction* (London: Routledge, 2008); Aaron A. Fox, *Real Country: Music and Language in Working-Class Culture* (Durham, NC: Duke University Press, 2004); Tony Bennett, Michael Emmison, and John Frow, *Accounting for Taste: Australian Everyday Cultures* (Cambridge: Cambridge University Press, 1999); Pierre Bourdieu, *Distinction: A Social Critique of the Judgement of Taste* (London: Routledge, 2010); Michael Denning, *Mechanic Accents: Dime Novels and Working Class Culture in America* (London: Verso, 1999); Jon M. Kingsdale, "The 'Poor Man's Club': Social Functions of the Urban Working-Class Saloon," *American Quarterly* 25, no. 4 (1973): pp. 472–489; Anoop Nayak, "Last of the 'Real Geordies'? White Masculinities and the Subcultural Response to Deindustrialization," *Environment and Planning D: Society and Space* 21, no. 1 (2003): pp. 7–25; Kathy Peiss, *Cheap Amusements: Working Women and Leisure in Turn-of-the-Century New York* (Philadelphia: Temple University Press, 1986); Roy Rosenzweig, *Eight Hours for What We Will: Workers and Leisure in an Industrial City, 1870–1920* (Cambridge: Cambridge University Press, 1983); Mike Savage et al., "A New Model of Social Class? Findings from the BBC's Great British Class Survey Experiment," *Sociology* 47, no. 2 (2013): pp. 219–250.

23. See Mike Savage, "Working-Class Identities in the 1960s: Revisiting the Affluent Worker Study," *Sociology* 39, no. 5 (2005): pp. 929–946.

24. See Larry M. Bartels, *Unequal Democracy: The Political Economy of the New Gilded Age* (New York: Russell Sage Foundation, 2008), pp. 67–68.

25. Savage, "Working-Class Identities in the 1960s."

26. Owen Jones, *Chavs: The Demonization of the Working Class* (London: Verso, 2011).

27. E. P. Thompson, *The Making of the English Working Class* (New York: Vintage, 1963).

28. Peter Laslett, *The World We Have Lost* (London: Methuen, 1971), pp. 53–54.

29. Monica McDermott, *Working-Class White: The Making and Unmaking of Race Relations* (Berkeley: University of California Press, 2006), pp. 38–49; Ofer Sharone, "Why Do Unemployed Americans Blame Themselves while Israelis Blame the System?" *Social Forces* 91, no. 4 (2013): pp. 1429–1450.

30. "Moving on Up: Why Do Some Americans Leave the Bottom of the Economic Ladder, but Not Others?" Pew Charitable Trusts, November 7, 2013, http://www.pewstates.org/research/reports/moving-on-up-85899518104.

31. Douglas Massey, *Categorically Unequal: The American Stratification System* (New York: Russell Sage Foundation, 2007).

32. Sean F. Reardon, "The Widening Achievement Gap between the Rich and the Poor: New Evidence and Possible Explanations," in *Whither Opportunity? Rising Inequality, Schools, and Children's Life Chances*, edited by Greg J. Duncan and Richard J. Murnane (New York: Russell Sage Foundation, 2001), pp. 91–116.

33. Robert D. Putnam, Carl B. Frederick, and Kaisa Snellman, "Growing Class Gaps in Social Connectedness among American Youth," in *The Saguaro Seminar: Civic Engagement in America* (Cambridge, MA: Harvard Kennedy School of Government, 2012).

34. Ibid.

35. Pew, "Moving on Up."

36. Ibid.

37. Kjartan Páll Sveinsson, ed., *Who Cares about the White Working Class?* (London: Runnymede Trust, 2009).

38. Abramowitz and Teixeira, "The Decline of the White Working Class," pp. 394–395.

39. Ibid.

40. Ibid.

41. Miles Corak, "Income Inequality, Equality of Opportunity, and Intergenerational Mobility," *Journal of Economic Perspectives* 27, no. 3 (2013): pp. 79–102; OECD, *Economic Policy Reforms: Going for Growth* (Paris: OECD, 2010).

42. Raj Chetty et al., "Is the United States Still a Land of Opportunity? Recent Trends in Intergenerational Mobility," National Bureau of Economic Research Working Paper 19844 (2014).

43. National Equity Panel, "An Anatomy of Economic Inequality in the UK: Report of the National Equity Panel," 2010, http://news.bbc.co.uk/2/shared/bsp/hi/pdfs/27_01_10_inequalityfull.pdf.

44. Bob Usherwood, *Equity and Excellence in the Public Library: Why Ignorance Is Not Our Heritage* (Hampshire, UK: Ashgate, 2007).

45. See Jones, *Chavs*; Matt Wray, *Not Quite White: White Trash and the Boundaries of Whiteness* (Durham, NC: Duke University Press, 2006).

46. Jones, *Chavs*; Wray, *Not Quite White*.

47. Charles Murray, *Coming Apart: The State of White America, 1960–2010* (New York: Random House, 2012).

48. Ibid., pp. 171, 176.

49. Ibid., pp. 172–173.

50. See Ross Douthat and Reihan Salam, *Grand New Party* (New York: Doubleday, 2008); W. Bradford Wilcox and Elizabeth Marquardt, eds. *When Marriage Disappears: The New Middle America* (West Chester, PA: Broadway Publications, 2011).

51. Murray, *Coming Apart*, pp. 161–162; see also Douthat and Salam, *Grand New Party*, p. 134.

52. Kevin Willamson, "The Father-Führer," *National Review*, March 28, 2016, http://www.nationalreview.com/nrd/articles/432569/father-f-hrer.

53. Jones, *Chavs*; Murray, *Coming Apart*.

54. See Fevisa Demie and Kirstin Lewis, *Raising the Achievement of White Working Class Pupils: Barriers and School Strategies* (London: Lambeth Council, 2010); Jones, *Chavs*.

55. Ahmed White, *The Last Great Strike: Little Steel, the CIO, and the Struggle for Labor Rights in New Deal America* (Berkeley: University of California Press, 2016), pp. 1, 36–38.

56. See Ellen Griffith Spears, *Baptized in PCBs: Race, Pollution, and Justice in an All-American Town* (Chapel Hill: University of North Carolina Press, 2014).

57. See Lori R. Armstrong et al., "Colorectal Carcinoma Mortality among Appalachian Men and Women, 1969–1999," *Cancer* 101, no. 12 (2004): pp. 2851–2858; Joel A. Halverson, Elizabeth Barnett, and Michele Casper, "Geographic Disparities in Heart Disease and Stroke Mortality among Black and White Populations in the Appalachian Region," *Ethnicity and Disease* 12, no. 3 (2002): pp. 82–91; Elizabeth L. McGarvey et al., "Health Disparities between Appalachian and Non-Appalachian Counties in Virginia USA," *Journal of Community Health* 36 (2011): pp. 348–356; Vanessa L. Short, Reena Oza-Frank, and Elizabeth J. Conrey, "Preconception Health Indicators: A Comparison between Non-Appalachian and Appalachian Women," *Maternal and Child Health Journal* 16, no. 2 (2012): pp. 238–249.

58. See Susan Starr Sered and Rushika Fernandopulle, *Uninsured in America: Life and Death in the Land of Opportunity* (Berkeley: University of California Press, 2005), p. 6.

59. Anne Case and Angus Deaton, "Rising Morbidity and Mortality in Midlife among White Non-Hispanic Americans in the 21st Century," *PNAS* 112, no. 49 (2015) : pp. 15078–15083.

60. Ibid.

61. Ibid.

62. Ibid., p. 15079.

63. Ibid., p. 15080.

64. Rose A. Rudd et al., "Increases in Drug and Opioid Overdose Deaths—United States, 2000–2014," *Morbidity and Mortality Weekly Report* 64, no. 50 (2016): pp. 1378–1382.

65. Ibid.

66. Todd Kerensky and Alexander Y. Walley, "Opioid Overdose Prevention and Naloxone Rescue Kits: What We Know and What We Don't Know," *Addiction Science and Clinical Practice* 12, no. 4 (2017).

67. Theodore J. Cicero et al., "The Changing Face of Heroin Use in the United States: A Retrospective Analysis of the Past 50 Years," *JAMA* 71, no. 7 (2014): pp. 821–826.

68. Ibid.

69. Michael J. Zoorob and Jason L. Salemi, "Bowling Alone, Dying Together: The Role of Social Capital in Mitigating the Drug Overdose Epidemic in the United States," *Drug and Alcohol Dependence* 173 (2017): pp. 1–9. See also Victor Tan Chen, "All Hollowed Out: The Lonely Poverty of America's White Working Class," *The Atlantic*, January 16, 2016, https://www.theatlantic.com/business/archive/2016/01/white-working-class-poverty/424341/.

70. See Linda McDowell, *Redundant Masculinities? Employment Change and White Working Class Youth* (Oxford: Blackwell, 2003); Claire Cain Miller, "Republican Men Say It's a Better Time to Be a Woman Than a Man," *New York Times*, January 17, 2017, https://www.nytimes.com/2017/01/17/upshot/republican-men-say-its-a-better-time-to-be-a-woman-than-a-man.html; Anoop Nayak, "Displaced Masculinities: Chavs, Youth and Class in the Post-Industrial City," *Sociology* 40 (2006): pp. 817–820, 828; Reg Theriault, *The Unmaking of the American Working Class* (New York: New Press, 2003), p. 79.

71. David H. Autor, David Dorn, and Gordon H. Hanson, "When Work Disappears: Manufacturing Decline and the Falling Marriage-Market Value of Men," National Bureau of Economic Research Working Paper W23173 (2017).

72. Ibid.

73. Naomi Farber and Julie E. Miller-Cribbs, "Violence in the Lives of Rural, Southern, and Poor White Women," *Violence against Women* 20, no. 5 (2014): pp. 517–538, 531.

74. See David Rosner and Gerald Markowitz, "The Struggle over Employee Benefits: The Role of Labor in Influencing Modern Health Policy," *Milbank Quarterly* 81, no. 1 (2003): 45–73.

75. Sered and Fernandopulle, *Uninsured in America*, p. 4.

76. Ibid., pp. 4–5.

77. Theriault, *The Unmaking of the American Working Class*, p. 201.
78. Sered and Fernandopulle, *Uninsured in America*, pp. 4–6.
79. See Ronald Brownstein, "Will Blue-Collar Whites Change Their Minds about Obamacare?" *The Atlantic*, January 5, 2017, https://www.theatlantic.com/politics/archive/2017/01/blue-collar-whites-obamacare/512159; Vann R. Newkirk II, "Simply Repealing Obamacare Will Hurt the White Working Class," *The Atlantic*, November 22, 2016, https://www.theatlantic.com/politics/archive/2016/11/trump-healthcare-plan-working-class-whites/508325.
80. Ronald Brownstein, "Eclipsed: Why the White Working Class Is the Most Alienated and Pessimistic Group in American Society," *National Journal*, May 26, 2011, http://www.nationaljournal.com/columns/political-connections/white-working-class-americans-see-future-as-gloomy-20110526.
81. Marisa Abrajano and Zoltan L. Hajnal, *White Backlash: Immigration, Race, and American Politics* (Princeton, NJ: Princeton University Press, 2014); Kaufmann, *The Rise and Fall of Anglo-America*.
82. Rishi Sunak and Saratha Rajeswaran, "A Portrait of Modern Britain" (London: Policy Exchange, 2014), p. 6.
83. "Millennials Outnumber Baby Boomers and Are Far More Diverse, Census Bureau Reports," US Census Bureau, June 25, 2015, http://www.census.gov/newsroom/press-releases/2015/cb15-113.html.
84. Audrey Singer, "Contemporary Immigrant Gateways in Historical Perspective," *Daedalus* 142, no. 3 (2013).
85. Abramowitz and Teixeira, "The Decline of the White Working Class," p. 395.
86. Case and Deaton, "Rising Morbidity and Mortality."
87. British Election Study, 2015.
88. American National Election Studies (ANES), 2016.
89. British Election Study, 2015.
90. ANES, 2016.

91. Paul Hudson, "80 Years of Ford at Dagenham," *The Telegraph*, May 15, 2009, http://www.telegraph.co.uk/motoring/classiccars/5318900/80-years-of-Ford-at-Dagenham.html.

92. Terry F. Buss and Steven Redburn, *Shutdown at Youngstown: Public Policy for Mass Unemployment* (Albany: State University of New York Press, 1983), p. 2; Sherry Lee Linkon and John Russo, *Steeltown USA: Work and Memory in Youngstown* (Lawrence: University Press of Kansas, 2002), p. 38.

93. Ibid.

94. Ibid.

## Chapter 2

1. Ashley Jardina, *The New Role of White Identity in American Politics* (unpublished book manuscript, 2017).

2. Claudine Gay, Jennifer Hochschild, and Ariel White, "Americans' Belief in Linked Fate: Does the Measure Capture the Concept?" *Journal of Race, Ethnicity, and Politics* 1, no. 1 (2016): pp. 117–144, 120.

3. American National Election Studies (ANES), 2017; 2016 Collaborative Multiracial Post-Election Survey (CMPS), http://www.latinodecisions.com/recent-polls/cmps-2016/.

4. Gay, Hochschild, and White, "Americans' Belief in Linked Fate," p. 120.

5. Liam Kennedy, "Alien Nation: White Male Paranoia and Imperial Culture in the United States," *Journal of American Studies* 30, no. 1 (1996): pp. 87–100, 88.

6. Joel Olson, "Whiteness and the Participation-Inclusion Dilemma," *Political Theory* 30, no. 3 (2002): pp. 384–409, 388.

7. Geoff Dench, Kate Gavron, and Michael Young, *The New East End: Kinship, Race and Conflict* (London: Profile, 2009); Eric P. Kaufmann, *The Rise and Fall of Anglo-America* (Cambridge, MA: Harvard University Press, 2004).

8. Nicholas Carnes, "Does the Numerical Underrepresentation of the Working Class in Congress Matter?" *Legislative Studies Quarterly* 37, no. 1 (2012): pp. 5–34.

9. Peter Whoriskey, "Growing Wealth Widens Distance between Lawmakers and Constituents," *Washington Post*, December 26, 2011, http://www.washingtonpost.com/business/economy/growing-wealth-widens-distance-between-lawmakers-and-constituents/2011/12/05/gIQAR7D6IP_story.html.

10. Christian Joppke, "Minority Rights for Immigrants? Multiculturalism versus Antidiscrimination," *Israel Law Review* 43 (2010): pp. 49–56, 49, 50.

11. Louis Wirth, "The Problem of Minority Groups," in *The Science of Man in the World Crisis*, edited by Ralph Linton (New York: Columbia University Press, 1940), p. 347.

12. Martin Gilens, "Inequality and Democratic Responsiveness," *Public Opinion Quarterly* 69, no. 5 (2005): pp. 778–796, 788–789.

13. Nathan Kelly and Peter Enns, "Inequality and the Dynamics of Public Opinion: The Self-Reinforcing Link between Economic Inequality and Mass Preferences," *American Journal of Political Science* 54, no. 4 (2010): pp. 855–870, 856.

14. Gary Freeman, "Immigration, Diversity, and Welfare Chauvinism," *Forum* 7, no. 3 (2009): Article 7, pp. 2–5; Martin Gilens, *Why Americans Hate Welfare: Race, Media and the Politics of Antipoverty Policy* (Cambridge: Cambridge University Press, 1999), p. 113; Michèle Lamont, *The Dignity of Working Men: Morality and the Boundaries of Race, Class, and Immigration* (New York: Russell Sage Foundation, 2000); Jeroen Van der Waal, Peter Achterbergand, and Wim Van Oorschot, "Why Are in Some European Countries Immigrants Considered Less Entitled to Welfare?" (paper presented at the Norface Conference, London, April 6–9, 2011), p. 16.

15. Andrew Gelman, *Red State, Blue State, Rich State, Poor State: Why Americans Vote the Way They Do* (Princeton, NJ: Princeton University Press, 2008), pp. 18, 83; but see Larry M. Bartels, *Unequal Democracy: The Political Economy of the New Gilded Age* (New York: Russell Sage Foundation, 2008); Ronald Inglehart and Christian Welzel, *Modernization, Cultural*

*Change, and Democracy: The Human Development Sequence* (Cambridge: Cambridge University Press, 2005), p. 3.

16. Bill Bishop, *The Big Sort: Why the Clustering of Like-Minded America Is Tearing Us Apart* (New York: Houghton Mifflin, 2008), pp. 11, 135.

17. John Jost and Orsolya Hunyady, "Antecedents and Consequences of System-Justifying Ideologies," *Current Directions in Psychological Science* 14, no. 5 (2005) : pp. 260–265, 263–264.

18. Ibid., p. 262; John Jost, Mahzarin Banaji, and Brian Nosek, "A Decade of System Justification Theory: Accumulated Evidence of Conscious and Unconscious Bolstering of the Status Quo," *Political Psychology* 25, no. 6 (2004): pp. 881–919, 894, 912.

19. Michael Zweig, *The Working Class Majority: America's Best Kept Secret* (Ithaca, NY: ILR Press, 2000), p. 61.

20. Peter Tyler Fenton et al., *Why Do Neighbourhoods Stay Poor? Deprivation, Place and People in Birmingham: A Report to the Barrow Cadbury Trust* (Cambridge: Cambridge Center for Housing and Planning Research, 2010).

21. Michael Dawson, *Behind the Mule: Race and Class in African-American Politics* (Princeton, NJ: Princeton University Press, 1995), p. 81; Lamont, *The Dignity of Working Men.*

22. See Julian B. Rotter, "Internal versus External Control of Reinforcement: A Case History of a Variable," *American Psychologist* 45, no. 4 (1990): pp. 489–493.

23. Matt Wray, *Not Quite White: White Trash and the Boundaries of Whiteness* (Durham, NC: Duke University Press, 2006), p. 134.

24. Claude M. Steele, "A Threat in the Air: How Stereotypes Shape Intellectual Identity and Performance," *American Psychologist* 52, no. 6 (1997): pp. 613–629.

25. John Zaller, *The Nature and Origins of Mass Opinion* (Cambridge: Cambridge University Press, 1992).

26. Matthew Goodwin, *Right Response: Understanding and Countering Populist Extremism in Europe* (London: Chatham House Report, 2011).

27. Robert Ford and Matthew Goodwin, "Angry White Men: Individual and Contextual Prediction of Support for the British National Party," *Political Studies* 58 (2010): pp. 1–25, 3.

28. Paul Sniderman, Louk Hagendoorn, and Markus Prior, "Predisposing Factors and Situational Triggers: Exclusionary Reactions to Immigrant Minorities," *American Political Science Review* 98, no. 1 (2004): pp. 3–49.

29. Terri Givens, *Voting Radical Right in Western Europe* (Cambridge: Cambridge University Press, 2005) .

30. Ibid., p. 100.

31. Loren Collingwood, Tyler Reny, and Ali Valenzuela, "Switching for Trump: Immigration, Not Economics, Explains Shift in White Working Class Behavior in 2016," Working Paper (2017); see also John Sides, *Race, Religion, and Immigration in 2016* (Voter Study Group, 2017).

32. E.g., Jack Citrin, Amy Lerman, Michael Murakami, and Kathryn Pearson, "Testing Huntington: Is Hispanic Immigration a Threat to American Identity?," *Perspectives on Politics* 5, no. 1 (2007): pp. 31–48.

**Chapter 3**

1. Gabe Lenz, *Follow the Leader? How Voters Respond to Politicians' Policies and Performance* (Chicago: University of Chicago Press, 2012); Michael Tesler, 2015. "Priming Predispositions and Changing Policy Positions: An Account of When Mass Opinion Is Primed or Changed," *American Journal of Political Science* 59, no. 4 (2015): pp. 806–824.

2. Daniel J. Tichenor, *Dividing Lines: The Politics of Immigration Control in America* (Princeton, NJ: Princeton University Press, 2002).

3. See Nancy DiTomaso, *The American Non-Dilemma: Racial Inequality without Racism* (New York: Russell Sage Foundation, 2012).

4. Michèle Lamont, *The Dignity of Working Men: Morality and the Boundaries of Race, Class, and Immigration* (New York: Russell Sage Foundation, 2000), pp. 131–141.

5. Brian Steensland, *The Failed Welfare Revolution: America's Struggle over Guaranteed Income Policy* (Princeton, NJ: Princeton University Press, 2008).

6. Michael K. Brown, *Race, Money, and the American Welfare State* (Ithaca, NY: Cornell University Press, 1991); Donald R. Kinder and Cindy D. Kam, *Us against Them: Ethnocentric Foundations of American Opinion* (Chicago: University of Chicago Press, 2009), pp. 182–191.

7. Joseph R. Gusfield, *Symbolic Crusade: Status Politics and the American Temperance Movement* (Urbana: University of Illinois Press, 1963), p. 15.

8. Matthew Goodwin and Oliver Heath, "Brexit Vote Explained: Poverty, Low Skills, and Lack of Opportunity," Joseph Rowntree Foundation, August 31, 2016, http://www.jrf.org.uk/report/brexit-vote-explained-poverty-low-skills-and-lack-opportunities.

9. Alan Travis, "Fear of Immigration Drove the Leave Victory—Not Immigration Itself," *The Guardian*, June 24, 2016, http://www.theguardian.com/politics/2016/jun/24/voting-details-show-immigration-fears-were-paradoxical-but-decisive.

10. Robert Ford and Matthew Goodwin, "Britain after Brexit: A Nation Divided," *Journal of Democracy* 28, no. 1 (2017): pp. 17–30, 20.

11. Sascha O. Becker, Thiemo Fetzer, and Dennis Novy, "Who Voted for Brexit? A Comprehensive District-Level Analysis" (University of Warwick Working Paper, 2017), p. 19.

12. Goodwin and Heath, "Brexit Vote Explained."

13. Italo Colantone and Piero Stanig, "The Real Reason the UK Voted for Brexit? Jobs Lost to Chinese Competition," *Washington Post*, July 7, 2016, http://www.washingtonpost.com/news/monkey-cage/wp/2016/07/07/the-real-reason-the-u-k-voted-for-brexit-economics-not-identity.

14. Travis, "Fear of Immigration Drove the Leave Victory."

15. Ford and Goodwin, "Britain after Brexit," p. 21.

16. Ibid., p. 22.

17. Ibid., pp. 23–24.

18. Josh Levin, "The Welfare Queen," *Slate*, December 19, 2013, http://www.slate.com/articles/news_and_politics/history/2013/12/linda_taylor_welfare_queen_ronald_reagan_made_her_a_notorious_american_villain.html.

19. Joshua J. Dyck and Laura S. Hussey, "The End of Welfare as We Know It? Durable Attitudes in a Changing Information Environment," *Public Opinion Quarterly* 72, no. 3 (2008): pp. 589–618, 604.

20. Martin Gilens, *Why Americans Hate Welfare: Race, Media and the Politics of Antipoverty Policy* (Cambridge: Cambridge University Press, 1999).

21. Christian Albrekt Larsen, "The Poor of the Mass Media," *Poverty* 148 (2014): pp. 14–17, 15.

22. Ibid.

23. Richard M. Coughlin, "Welfare Myths and Stereotypes," in *Reforming Welfare: Limits, Lessons, and Choices*, edited by Richard M. Coughlin (Albuquerque: New Mexico University Press, 1989), pp. 79–106, 83.

24. Jens Hainmueller and Michel J. Hiscox, "Attitudes toward Highly Skilled and Low-Skilled Immigration: Evidence from a Survey Experiment," *American Political Science Review* 104, no. 1 (2010): pp. 61–84.

25. Steven A. Camarota, *Welfare Use by Immigrant and Native Households* (Center for Immigration Studies, 2015).

26. Laura Reston, "Immigrants Don't Drain Welfare. They Fund It," *New Republic*, September 3, 2015, http://newrepublic.com/article/122714/immigrants-dont-drain-welfare-they-fund-it; Alex Nowrasteh, "CIS Exaggerates the Cost of Immigrant Welfare Use," Cato Institute, May 10, 2016, https://www.cato.org/blog/cis-exaggerates-cost-immigrant-welfare-use.

27. Paul Bedard, "Report: America Attracting Poor, Uneducated Immigrants," *Washington Examiner*, September 10, 2015, http://www.washingtonexaminer.com/

report-america-attracting-poor-uneducated-immigrants/
article/2571730; Steven Camarota, "Heavy Welfare Use by
Legal Immigrants—Yes, *Legal* Immigrants," *National Review*,
September 10, 2015, http://www.nationalreview.com/
article/423780/-immigrants-welfare-use-legal; Alen Gomez,
"Report: More Than Half of Immigrants on Welfare," *USA
Today*, September 2, 2015, http://www.usatoday.com/story/
news/nation/2015/09/01/immigrant-welfare-use-report
/71517072; Caroline May, "Legal Immigrant Households
Account for 75 Percent of Immigrant Welfare Use,"
*Breitbart*, September 9, 2015, http://www.breitbart.com/
big-government/2015/09/09/legal-immigrant-households-
account-for-75-percent-of-immigrant-welfare-use; Adam Shaw,
"About Half of Immigrant Households on Welfare, Report
Says," *Fox News*, September 2, 2015; http://www.foxnews.
com/politics/2015/09/02/half-immigrant-households-on-
welfare-report-says.html.

28. "Refugees in Britain: The Facts behind the Headlines," *The
Week*, September 3, 2015, http://www.theweek.co.uk/refugee-
crisis/65056/refugees-in-britain-the-facts-behind-the-headlines.

29. David Cameron, letter to Donald Tusk, November 10,
2015, http://www.gov.uk/government/uploads/system/
uploads/attachment_data/file/475679/Donald_Tusk_letter.
pdf.

30. Alberto Alesina, Edward Glaeser, and Bruce Sacerdote, "Why
Doesn't the US Have a European-Style Welfare System?"
National Bureau of Economic Research Working Paper 8524
(2001).

31. Ibid.

32. Robert A. Moffitt and Peter T. Gottschalk, "Ethnic and Racial
Differences in Welfare Receipt in the United States," in
*America Becoming: Racial Trends and Their Consequences, Vol.
II*, edited by Neil J. Smelser, William Julius Wilson, and Faith
Mitchell (Washington, DC: National Academy Press, 2001),
pp. 152–173, 153.

33. Suzanne Macartney, Alemayehu Bishaw, and Kayla Fontenot, *Poverty Rates for Selected Detailed Race and Hispanic Groups by State and Place: 2007–2011* (US Census, 2013), http://www.census.gov/prod/2013pubs/acsbr11-17.pdf.

34. Moffitt and Gottschalk, "Ethnic and Racial Differences," p. 169.

35. Kelsey Farson Gray, "Characteristics of Supplemental Nutrition Assistance Program Households: Fiscal Year 2013" (Alexandria, VA: US Department of Agriculture, Food and Nutrition Service, Office of Policy Support, 2014), Table A-21, https://www.fns.usda.gov/sites/default/files/ops/Characteristics2013.pdf.

36. "Annual Statistical Supplement, 2010" (Social Security Administration, 2010), Table 5.A1, https://www.ssa.gov/policy/docs/statcomps/supplement/2010/5a.html.

37. Marios Michaelides and Peter R. Mueser, "Recent Trends in the Characteristics of Unemployment Insurance Recipients," *Monthly Labor Review* (July 2012): Table 1.

38. "Characteristics and Financial Circumstances of TANF Recipients, Fiscal Year 2013" (US Department of Health and Human Services, Administration for Children and Families, 2015), Table 10, https://www.acf.hhs.gov/sites/default/files/ofa/tanf_characteristics_fy2013.pdf.

39. Ibid., Table 19.

40. Mark Easton, "Work, Benefits and Ethnicity," *BBC News*, November 12, 2010, http://www.bbc.co.uk/blogs/thereporters/markeaston/2010/11/work_benefits_and_ethnicity.html.

41. 8 USC §§ 1612, 1641.

42. Younghee Lim and Stella M. Resko, "Immigrants' Use of Welfare after Welfare Reform: Cross-Group Comparison," *Journal of Poverty* 6, no. 2 (2002): pp. 63–82.

43. Kevin F. McCarthy and R. Burciaga Valdez, *Current and Future Effects of Mexican Immigration in California* (RAND Corporation, 1986).

44. George J. Borjas and Lynette Hilton, "Immigration and the Welfare State: Immigrant Participation in Means-Tested Entitlement Programs," *Quarterly Journal of Economics* 111, no. 2 (1996): pp. 575–604; George J. Borjas and Stephen J. Trejo, "Immigrant Participation in the Welfare System," *Industrial and Labor Relations Review* 44, no. 2 (1991): pp. 195–211.

45. George J. Borjas, "Welfare Reform and Immigrant Participation in Welfare Programs," *International Migration Review* 36, no. 4 (2002): pp. 1093–1123.

46. Stephen Drinkwater and Catherine Robinson, "Welfare Participation by Immigrants in the UK," *International Journal of Manpower* 34, no. 2 (2013): pp. 100–112, 102.

47. Richard Keen and Ross Turner, *Statistics on Migrants and Benefits* (House of Commons Library, Briefing Paper, Number CBP 7445, February 8, 2016).

48. Herbert Brucker et al., "Welfare State Provision," in *Immigration Policy and the Welfare State*, edited by Tito Boeri, Gordon H. Hanson, and Barry McCormick (Oxford: Oxford University Press, 2002).

49. Donald J. Trump, Republican nomination acceptance speech (2016), https://assets.donaldjtrump.com/DJT_Acceptance_Speech.pdf.

50. Ben Schreckinger, "Donald Trump Storms Phoenix," *Politico*, July 11, 2015, http://www.politico.com/story/2015/07/donald-trump-storms-phoenix-119989.

51. E.g., Aviva Chomsky, *They Take Our Jobs!* (Boston: Beacon Press, 2007), p. 3.

52. "President Bush's Plan for Comprehensive Immigration Reform" (White House, 2007), http://georgewbush-whitehouse.archives.gov/stateoftheunion/2007/initiatives/immigration.html.

53. Federation for Immigration Reform, "Illegal Aliens Taking US Jobs," Fair Immigration Reform, accessed January 20, 2017, http://www.fairus.org/issue/illegal-aliens-taking-u-s-jobs.

54. Shaun Firkser, "Nigel Farage Blames Immigrants for Taking Jobs and Ruining Children's Lives," *Daily Mirror*, August 27, 2015, http://www.mirror.co.uk/news/video/nigel-farage-blames-immigrants-taking-6329603.

55. Fraser Nelson, "Nigel Farage Has Just Been Rumbled on Immigration," *The Spectator*, June 10, 2016, http://blogs.spectator.co.uk/2016/06/tonight-nigel-farage-rumbled-immigration.

56. Michael Wilkinson, "Amber Rudd Vows to Stop Migrants 'Taking Jobs British People Could Do' and Force Companies to Reveal Number of Foreigners They Employ," *The Telegraph*, October 4, 2016, http://www.telegraph.co.uk/news/2016/10/04/jeremy-hunt-nhs-doctors-theresa-may-conservative-conference-live.

57. Peter Brimelow and Leslie Spencer, "When Quotas Replace Merit, Everybody Suffers," *Forbes*, February 15, 1993, pp. 80–102.

58. "Poll: Slim Majority Backs Same-Sex Marriage," *CBS News*, June 6, 2013, http://www.cbsnews.com/news/poll-slim-majority-backs-same-sex-marriage.

59. Drew Desilver, "Supreme Court Says States Can Ban Affirmative Action; 8 Already Have," *Pew Research Center*, April 22, 2014, http://www.pewresearch.org/fact-tank/2014/04/22/supreme-court-says-states-can-ban-affirmative-action-8-already-have.

60. Ibid.

61. Equality Act of 2010 (c. 15).

62. Ibid., § 159.

63. Chomsky, *They Take Our Jobs!*, p. 8.

64. Ibid., p. 205.

65. Rakesh Kochnar, "Growth in the Foreign-Born Workforce and Employment of the Native Born," *Pew Research Center*, August 10, 2006, http://www.pewhispanic.org/2006/08/10/growth-in-the-foreign-born-workforce-and-employment-of-the-native-born.

66. Ibid.
67. E.g., George J. Borjas, Richard B. Freeman, and Lawrence F. Katz, "How Much Do Immigration and Trade Affect Labor Market Outcomes?" (Brookings Papers on Economic Activity, 1997); George J. Borjas, "The Analytics of the Wage Effect of Immigration," *IZA Journal of Migration* 2 (2013): pp. 1–25.
68. George J. Borjas, "The Economics of Immigration," *Journal of Economic Literature* 32 (1994): pp. 1667–1717, 1698.
69. Francine D. Blau and Christopher Mackie, eds., *The Economic and Fiscal Consequences of Immigration* (Washington, DC: National Academies Press, 2016) .
70. Ibid., p. 149.
71. Ibid., p. 150.
72. Ibid., p. 202.
73. Ibid., p. 203.
74. Ibid., p. 204.
75. Ibid.
76. Ibid.
77. Ibid., p. 205.
78. Ibid., p. 202.
79. Erik Brynjolfsson and Andrew McAfee, *Race against the Machine* (Lexington, MA: Digital Frontier, 2011).
80. Francesco D'Amuri and Giovanni Peri, "Immigration, Jobs, and Employment Protection: Evidence from Europe before and after the Great Recession," *Journal of the European Economic Association* 12, no. 2 (2014): pp. 432–464.
81. Dean Hochlaf and Ben Franklin, *Immigration: Encourage or Deter?* (London: International Longevity Centre, 2016).
82. "Unemployment," Office for National Statistics, http:// www.ons.gov.uk/employmentandlabourmarket/ peoplenotinwork/unemployment.
83. Charlotte Steeh and Maria Krysan, "Affirmative Action and the Public, 1970–1995," *Public Opinion Quarterly* 60, no. 1 (1996): pp. 128–158, 139–140.

84. Jennifer Hochschild, "Affirmative Action as a Culture War," in *A Companion to Racial and Ethnic Studies*, edited by David Theo Goldberg and John Solomos (Malden, MA: Wiley-Blackwell, 2002), pp. 282–303.

85. As quoted by Angie Drobnic Holan, "In Context: Hillary Clinton and the 'Basket of Deplorables,'" *Politifact*, September 11, 2016, http://www.politifact.com/truth-o-meter/article/2016/sep/11/context-hillary-clinton-basket-deplorables.

86. Ibid.

87. Data Team, "How Deplorable Are Trump Supporters?" *The Economist*, September 13, 2016, http://www.economist.com/blogs/graphicdetail/2016/09/daily-chart-8.

88. *Ten Days After: Harassment and Intimidation in the Aftermath of the Election* (Southern Poverty Law Center, 2016).

89. Jon Kelly, "In Numbers: Has Britain Really Become More Racist?" *BBC News*, August 10, 2016, http://www.bbc.com/news/magazine-36964916.

90. "Racism on the Rise in UK after Brexit Vote: Watchdog," *Al Jazeera*, August 20, 2016, http://www.aljazeera.com/news/2016/08/racism-rise-uk-brexit-vote-watchdog-160819093506647.html.

91. V. O. Key, *Southern Politics in State and Nation* (New York: Knopf, 1949).

92. Benjamin J. Newman, "Acculturating Contexts and Anglo Opposition to Immigration in the United States," *American Journal of Political Science* 57, no. 2 (2012): pp. 374–390; Benjamin J. Newman, "Foreign Language Exposure, Cultural Threat, and Opposition to Immigration," *Political Psychology* 33, no. 5 (2012): pp. 635–657.

93. Donald P. Green, Dara Z. Strolovitch, and Janelle S. Wong, "Defended Neighborhoods, Integration, and Racially Motivated Crime," *American Journal of Sociology* 104, no. 2 (1998): pp. 372–403.

94. "US Immigrant Population and Share over Time, 1850–Present" (Migration Policy Institute, 2015), http://

www.migrationpolicy.org/programs/data-hub/charts/
immigrant-population-over-time.

95. "Migrants in the UK: An Overview" (Migration
    Observatory at the University of Oxford, 2016), http://
    www.migrationobservatory.ox.ac.uk/resources/briefings/
    migrants-in-the-uk-an-overview.

96. Hubert M. Blalock, *Toward a Theory of Minority Group Relations*
    (New York: Wiley and Sons, 1967); Robert D. Putnam, "*E
    Pluribus Unum*: Diversity and Community in the Twenty-
    First Century," *Scandinavian Political Studies* 30, no. 2
    (2007): pp. 137–174.

97. Jack Citrin et al., "Public Opinion toward Immigration
    Reform: The Role of Economic Motivations," *Journal of
    Politics* 59, no. 3 (1997): pp. 858–881; Jack Citrin, Beth
    Reingold, and Donald P. Green, "American Identity and
    the Politics of Ethnic Change," *Journal of Politics* 52, no. 4
    (1990): pp. 1124–1154.

98. Jens Hainmueller and Michael J. Hiscox, "Educated
    Preferences: Explaining Attitudes toward Immigration
    in Europe," *International Organization* 61 (2007): pp. 399–
    442; John Sides and Jack Citrin, "European Opinion
    about Immigration: The Role of Identities, Interests,
    and Information," *British Journal of Political Science* 37
    (2007): pp. 477–504.

99. Jens Hainmueller and Daniel J. Hopkins, "Public Attitudes
    toward Immigration," *Annual Review of Political Science* 17
    (2014): pp. 225–249.

100. Newman, "Acculturating Contexts," p. 375.

101. Thomas F. Pettigrew and Linda R. Tropp, "A Meta-Analytic
    Test of Intergroup Contact Theory," *Journal of Personality and
    Social Psychology* 90, no. 5 (2006): pp. 751–783.

102. Newman, "Acculturating Contexts," p. 376.

103. Shang E. Ha, "The Consequences of Multiracial Contexts
    on Public Attitudes toward Immigration," *Political Research
    Quarterly* 63, no. 1 (2010): pp. 29–42.

104. Ryan D. Enos and Noam Gidron, "Intergroup Behavioral Strategies as Contextually Determined: Experimental Evidence from Israel," *Journal of Politics* 78, no. 3 (2016): pp. 851–867.

105. Allison L. Skinner and Jacob E. Cheadle, "The 'Obama Effect'? Priming Contemporary Social Milestones Increases Implicit Racial Bias among Whites," *Social Cognition* 34, no. 6 (2016): pp. 544–558.

106. Susan Welch and Lee Sigelman, "The 'Obama Effect' and Racial Attitudes," *Annals of the American Academy of Political and Social Science* 634 (2011): pp. 207–220.

107. Ryan D. Enos, "The Causal Effect of Intergroup Contact on Exclusionary Attitudes," *Proceedings of the National Academy of Sciences of the United States of America* 111, no 10 (2014): pp. 3699–3704.

108. Joel Olson, "Whiteness and the Polarization of American Politics," *Political Research Quarterly* 61, no. 4 (2008): pp. 704–718, 704.

**Chapter 4**

1. "Election 2017 Results," BBC, http://www.bbc.com/news/election/2017/results.

2. Some content in this section first appeared in *Comparative Political Studies*. It is republished with permission from SAGE Publications.

3. Elisabeth Iversflaten, "What United Right-Wing Populists in Western Europe? Re-examining Grievance Mobilization Models in Seven Successful Cases," *Comparative Political Studies* 41, no. 1 (2008): pp. 3–23.

4. See Michael S. Lewis-Beck and Mary Stegmaier, "Economic Determinants of Electoral Outcomes," *Annual Review of Political Science* 3, no. 1 (2000): pp. 183–219.

5. Larry Bartels, "Ideology and Retrospection in Electoral Responses to the Great Recession," Working Paper (2011), http://www.vanderbilt.edu/csdi/research/CSDI_WP_04-2013.pdf.

6. See Christopher Hood, *The Art of the State: Culture, Rhetoric, and Public Management* (Oxford: Clarendon, 1998); Torben Iversen, "The Dynamics of the Welfare State Expansion: Trade Openness, De-Industrialization, and Partisan Politics," in *The New Politics of the Welfare State*, edited by Paul Pierson (Oxford: Oxford University Press, 2001).

7. Duane Swank and Hans-Georg Betz, "Globalization, the Welfare State and Right-Wing Populism in Western Europe," *Socio-Economic Review* (2003): pp. 215–245.

8. Richard Hofstadter, *The Paranoid Style in American Politics: And Other Essays* (New York: Vintage, 1967).

9. Donatella Della Porta and Yves Meny, eds., *Democracy and Corruption in Europe* (New York: Pinter, 1997).

10. Arim Abedi, "Challenges to Established Parties: The Effects of Party System Features on the Electoral Fortunes of Anti-Political-Establishment Parties," *European Journal of Political Research* 41, no. 4 (2002): pp. 551–583; Sylvia Bergh, "Democratic Decentralisation and Local Participation: A Review of Recent Research," *Development in Practice* 14, no. 6 (2004): pp. 780–790.

11. Terri Givens, *Voting Radical Right in Western Europe* (Cambridge: Cambridge University Press, 2005).

12. Daniel Bell, *The End of Ideology: On the Exhaustion of Political Ideas in the Fifties* (Cambridge, MA: Harvard University Press, 1988), pp. 103–123.

13. Thomas Byrne Edsall, "The Changing Shape of Power: A Realignment in Public Policy," in *The Rise and Fall of the New Deal Order, 1930–1980*, edited by Steve Fraser and Gary Gerstle (Princeton: Princeton University Press, 1989), pp. 264–293.

14. William Greider, *Who Will Tell the People: The Betrayal of American Democracy* (New York: Simon and Schuster, 1992).

15. Jacob S. Hacker and Paul Pierson, *Winner-Take-All Politics: How Washington Made the Rich Richer—And Turned Its Back on the Middle Class* (New York: Simon and Schuster, 2010).

16. Hofstadter, *The Paranoid Style in American Politics*.

17. Ibid.
18. Michael Tesler, *Post-Racial or Most-Racial? Race and Politics in the Obama Era* (Chicago: University of Chicago Press, 2016).
19. Kerem Ozan Kalkan, "What Differentiates Trump Supporters from Other Republicans? Ethnocentrism," *Washington Post*, February 28, 2016, http://www.washingtonpost.com/news/monkey-cage/wp/2016/02/28/what-differentiates-trump-supporters-from-other-republicans-ethnocentrism.
20. Amanda Taub, "The Rise of American Authoritarianism," *Vox*, March 1, 2016, http://www.vox.com/2016/3/1/11127424/trump-authoritarianism.
21. Hans-Georg Betz, "The New Politics of Resentment, Radical Right Wing Populist Parties in Western Europe," *Comparative Politics* 25 (1993): pp. 413–427.
22. Paul Sniderman, Louk Hagendoorn, and Markus Prior, "Predisposing Factors and Situational Triggers: Exclusionary Reactions to Immigrant Minorities," *American Political Science Review* 98, no. 1 (2004): pp. 3–49
23. Iversflaten, "What United Right-Wing Populists in Western Europe?"
24. Jens Hainmueller and Daniel J. Hopkins, "Public Attitudes toward Immigration," *Annual Review of Political Science* 17 (2014): pp. 225–249.
25. Cheryl I. Harris, "Whiteness as Property," *Harvard Law Review* 106, no. 8 (1993): pp. 1707–1791, 1713.
26. Joel Olson, "Whiteness and the Polarization of American Politics," *Political Research Quarterly* 61, no. 4 (2008): pp. 704–718, 708.
27. W. E. B. Du Bois, *Black Reconstruction in America* (New York: Harcourt, Brace and Co., 1935); Harris, "Whiteness as Property"; David R. Roedinger, *The Wages of Whiteness: Race and the Making of the American Working Class* (London: Verso, 1991).
28. Herbert Hiram Hyman, "The Psychology of Status," *Archives of Psychology* 269 (1942): pp. 5–91.

29. Nicholas Crafts and Gianni Toriolo, eds., *Economic Growth in Europe since 1945* (New York: Cambridge University Press, 1996); Stephen A. Marglin and Juliet B. Schor, *The Golden Age of Capitalism: Reinterpreting the Postwar Experience* (New York: Oxford University Press, 1992).

30. Keith T. Poole and Howard Rosenthal, *Congress: A Political-Economic History of Roll Call Voting* (New York: Oxford University Press, 1997).

31. Jim Sidanius and Felicia Pratto, *Social Dominance* (Cambridge: Cambridge University Press, 1999).

32. Harris, "Whiteness as Property," p. 1778.

33. Desmond S. King and Rogers M. Smith, "Racial Orders in American Political Development," *American Political Science Review* 99, no. 1 (2005): pp. 75–92.

34. "2016 Republican Presidential Nomination," *Real Clear Politics*, https://www.realclearpolitics.com/epolls/2016/president/us/2016_republican_presidential_nomination-3823.html#polls.

35. Some content in this section first appeared in POLITICO. It is republished with permission.

36. John Sides, *Race, Religion, and Immigration in 2016* (Voter Study Group, 2017).

37. Gabe Lenz, *Follow the Leader? How Voters Respond to Politicians' Policies and Performance* (Chicago: University of Chicago Press, 2012); John Zaller, *The Nature and Origins of Mass Opinion* (Cambridge: Cambridge University Press, 1992).

38. Sides, *Race, Religion, and Immigration in 2017*.

## Chapter 5

1. Sara Wallace Goodman, "Conceptualizing and Measuring Citizenship and Integration Policy: Past Lessons and New Approaches," *Comparative Political Studies* 48, no. 14 (2015): pp. 1905–1941; Sara Wallace Goodman, "Fortifying Citizenship: Policy Strategies for Civic Integration in Western Europe," *World Politics* 64, no. 4 (2012): pp. 659–698; Sara Wallace Goodman, "Integration Requirements for Integration's Sake? Identifying, Categorising and Comparing

Civic Integration Policies," *Journal of Ethnic and Migration Studies* 36, no. (2010): pp. 753–772.

2. Christian Joppke, "Beyond National Models: Civic Integration Policies for Immigrants in Western Europe," *West European Politics* 30, no. 1 (2007): pp. 1–22.

3. See William J. Blot et al., "Lung Cancer among Long-Term Steel Workers," *American Journal of Epidemiology* 117, no. 6 (1983): pp. 706–716; Susan M. Kennedy et al., "Acute Pulmonary Responses among Automobile Workers Exposed to Aerosols of Machining Fluids," *American Journal of Industrial Medicine* 15, no. 6 (1989): pp. 627–641.

4. Ahmed White, *The Last Great Strike: Little Steel, the CIO, and the Struggle for Labor Rights in New Deal America* (Berkeley: University of California Press, 2016), p. 23.

5. Ibid., p. 24.

6. Ibid.

7. Ibid.

8. See Richard Hoggart, *The Uses of Literacy: Aspects of Working-Class Life with Special Reference to Publications and Entertainments* (London: Penguin, 1958), pp. 336–338.

9. John P. Dean, "The Ghosts of Home Ownership," *Journal of Social Issues* 7, nos. 1–2 (1951): pp. 59–68, 59.

10. Stephanie Lawler, "Disgusted Subjects: The Making of Middle-Class Identities," *The Sociological Review* 53, no. 3 (2005): pp. 429–446.

11. Irving Tallman, "Working-Class Wives in Suburbia: Fulfillment or Crisis?" *Journal of Marriage and Family* 31, no. 1 (1969): pp. 65–72.

12. Andrew J. Cherlin, *Labor's Love Lost: The Rise and Fall of the Working-Class Family in America* (New York: Russell Sage Foundation, 2014), p. 4.

13. Ely Chinoy, "The Tradition of Opportunity and the Aspirations of Automobile Workers," *American Journal of Sociology* 57, no. 5 (1952): 453–459.

14. Becky M. Nicolaides, *My Blue Heaven: Life and Politics in the Working-Class Suburbs of Los Angeles, 1920–1965* (Chicago: University of Chicago Press, 2002), pp. 12–13, 28.

15. Ibid., pp. 12–13.
16. Ibid., p. 17.
17. James M. Allgren, "Youngstown's Fortunes Rose and Fell with the Steel Industry," in *Remembering Youngstown: Tales from the Mahoning Valley*, edited by Mark C. Peyko (Charleston, SC: History Press, 2009), pp. 35–40.
18. White, *The Last Great Strike*, pp. 43–44.
19. Ibid., pp. 16, 55.
20. Ibid., pp. 28–29.
21. Ibid., p. 26.
22. Ibid., p. 49.
23. Ibid., p. 283.
24. Stanley Aronowitz, *How Class Works: Power and Social Movement* (New Haven, CT: Yale University Press, 2003), pp. 23–24.
25. Ibid., p. 24; Reg Theriault, *The Unmaking of the American Working Class* (New York: New Press, 2003), pp. 41, 57.
26. Christian G. Appy, *Working-Class War: American Combat Soldiers and Vietnam* (Chapel Hill: University of North Carolina Press, 1993), pp. 6–7, 27.
27. Julie Bettie, "Class Dismissed? *Roseanne* and the Changing Face of Working-Class Iconography," *Social Text* 45 (1995): pp. 125–149.
28. Lisa A. Kirby, "Cowboys of the High Seas: Representations of Working-Class Masculinity on *Deadliest Catch*," *Journal of Popular Culture* 46, no. 1 (2013): pp. 109–118; James Rhodes, "Fighting for 'Respectability': Media Representations of the White, 'Working-Class' Male Boxing 'Hero,'" *Journal of Sport and Social Issues* 35, no. 4 (2011): pp. 350–376.
29. John Gray and David Block, "All Middle Class Now? Evolving Representations of the Working Class in the Neoliberal Era: The Case of ELT Textbooks," in *English Language Textbooks: Content, Consumption, Production*, edited by N. Hardwood (Basingstoke, UK: Palgrave Macmillan, 2014), pp. 45–71; Steph Lawler, "White Like Them: Whiteness and Anachronistic Space in Representations of the English White Working Class," *Ethnicities* 12, no. 4 (2012): pp. 409–426.

30. Lawler, "White Like Them."
31. Liam Kennedy, "Alien Nation: White Male Paranoia and Imperial Culture in the United States," *Journal of American Studies* 30, no. 1 (1996): pp. 87–100; Joel Olson, "Whiteness and the Participation-Inclusion Dilemma," *Political Theory* 30, no. 3 (2002): pp. 384–409.
32. See Cecily R. Hardaway, "Escaping Poverty and Securing Middle Class Status: How Race and Socioeconomic Status Shape Mobility Prospects for African Americans during the Transition to Adulthood," *Journal of Youth and Adolescence* 38, no. 2 (2009): pp. 242–256; Dayna Bowen Matthew, Richard V. Reeves, and Edward Rodrigue, "Health, Housing, and Racial Justice: An Agenda for the Trump Administration," *Economic Studies at Brookings Institute Report* (2017); Bhashkar Mazumder, "Black-White Differences in Intergenerational Economic Mobility in the United States," *Economic Perspectives* 38, no. 1 (2014): pp. 1–18.
33. Lillian B. Rubin, *Worlds of Pain: Life in the Working-Class Family* (New York: Basic Books, 1976), p. 29.
34. Richard G. Wilkinson, *Unhealthy Societies: The Afflictions of Inequality* (London: Routledge, 2002).
35. See Harris Beider, *White Working-Class Voices: Multiculturalism, Community-Building and Change* (Bristol, UK: Policy Press, 2015), pp. 143–146; Heather M. Dalmage, *Tripping on the Color Line: Black-White Multiracial Families in a Racially Divided World* (New Brunswick, NJ: Rutgers University Press, 2000), pp. 76–77; Lois Weis, *Class Reunion: The Remaking of the American White Working Class* (New York: Routledge, 2004), pp. 154–156.
36. "Tracking the Fortunes of the White Working-Class," *The Economist*, February 18, 2017, http://www.economist.com/news/united-states/21717068-our-new-labour-market-index-tracking-fortunes-white-working-class. For the general labor-force participation rate, see "Civilian Labor Force Participation Rate: Men," *Federal Reserve Bank of St. Louis*, last updated July 7, 2017, http://fred.stlouisfed.org/series/LNS11300001.

37. OECD, *Economic Polity Reforms: Going for Growth* (Paris: OECD), http://www.keepeek.com/Digital-Asset-Management/oecd/economics/economic-policy-reforms-2010_growth-2010-en; Thomas Piketty and Emmanuel Saez, "Income Inequality in the United States, 1913–1998," *Quarterly Journal of Economics* 118, no. 1 (2003): pp. 1–41.

38. Raj Chetty, "Socioeconomic Mobility in the United States: New Evidence and Policy Lessons," in *Shared Prosperity in America's Communities*, edited by Susan M. Wachter and Lei Ding (Philadelphia: University of Pennsylvania Press, 2016), pp. 7–19; see also Raj Chetty et al., "Is the United States Still a Land of Opportunity? Recent Trends in Intergenerational Mobility," National Bureau of Economic Research Working Paper 19844 (2014).

39. Miles Corak, "Income Inequality, Equality of Opportunity, and Intergenerational Mobility," *Journal of Economic Perspectives* 27, no. 3 (2013): pp. 79–102.

40. Chetty, "Socioeconomic Mobility in the United States,"  p. 12.

41. Ibid., p. 13.

42. Ibid., pp. 14–16.

43. Ibid., pp. 17–18. See also Raj Chetty et al., "How Does Your Kindergarten Classroom Affect Your Earnings? Evidence from Project Star," *Quarterly Journal of Economics* 126, no. 4 (2011): pp. 1593–1660.

44. Tara Bahrampour and Scott Clement, "White Working-Class Men Increasingly Falling Behind as College Becomes the Norm," *Washington Post*, October 5, 2016, http://www.washingtonpost.com/local/social-issues/white-working-class-men-increasingly-falling-behind-as-college-becomes-the-norm/2016/10/05/95610130-8a51-11e6-875e-2c1bfe943b66_story.html.

45. Douglas Massey, *Categorically Unequal: The American Stratification System* (New York: Russell Sage Foundation, 2007); Bhashkar Mazumder, "Is Intergenerational Mobility Lower Now Than in the Past?" (Chicago: Federal Reserve Bank of Chicago, 2012), p. 297; Robert D. Putnam, Carl

B. Frederick, and Kaisa Snellman, "Growing Class Gaps
in Social Connectedness among American Youth," in *The
Saguaro Seminar: Civic Engagement in America* (Cambridge,
MA: Harvard Kennedy School of Government, 2012).

46. Lois Weis, *Working Class without Work: High School Students in
a De-Industrializing Economy* (New York: Routledge, 1993), p. 3;
see also Diane Reay, "Beyond Consciousness?: The Psychic
Landscape of Social Class," *Sociology* 39, no. 5 (2005): pp. 911–
928; and April Sutton, Amanda Bosky, and Chandra Muller,
"Manufacturing Gender in the New Economy: High School
Training for Work in Blue-Collar Communities," *American
Sociological Review* 81, no. 4 (2016): pp. 720–748.

47. Vicki Smith and Esther B. Neuwirth, *The Good Temp* (Ithaca,
NY: Cornell University Press, 2008), p. 10.

48. Vicki Smith, "Enhancing Employability: Human, Cultural,
and Social Capital in an Era of Turbulent Unpredictability,"
*Human Relations* 63, no. 2 (2010): pp. 1–22, 8; see also Michael
Indegaard, "Retrainers as Labor Market Brokers: Constructing
Networks and Narratives in the Detroit Area," *Social Problems*
46 (1999): pp. 67–87; Smith and Neuwirth, *The Good Temp*.

49. Bourree Lam, "The Recovery's Geographic Disparities," *The
Atlantic*, February 26, 2016, http://www.theatlantic.com/
business/archive/2016/02/eig-distressed-communities/471177.

50. "Mapping Economic Distress," Economic Innovation Group,
accessed February 2016, http://eig.org/dci/infographics.

51. "US Cities Ranked by the Distressed Communities Index,"
Economic Innovation Group, accessed February 2016, http://
eig.org/dci/infographics#us-cities-ranked-by-the-dci.

52. "Economic Disparities in the United States," Economic
Innovation Group, accessed February 2016, http://eig.org/
dci/infographics#economic-disparities-in-the-united-states;
see also Bill Bishop, *The Big Sort: Why the Clustering of Like-
Minded America Is Tearing Us Apart* (New York: Houghton
Mifflin, 2008); Charles Murray, *Coming Apart: The State of
White America, 1960–2010* (New York: Random House, 2012).

53. Lam, "The Recovery's Geographic Disparities."

54. Chetty, "Socioeconomic Mobility in the United States," pp. 13–14; see also Raj Chetty, Nathaniel Hendren, and Lawrence F. Katz, "The Effects of Exposure to Better Neighborhoods on Children: New Evidence from the Moving to Opportunity Experiment," *American Economic Review* 106, no. 4 (2016): pp. 855–902; Raj Chetty and Nathaniel Hendren, "The Impacts of Neighborhoods on Intergenerational Mobility II: County-Level Estimates," National Bureau of Economic Research Working Paper W23002 (2016); Raj Chetty and Nathaniel Hendren, "The Impacts of Neighborhoods on Intergenerational Mobility: Childhood Exposure Effects and County-Level Estimates," Harvard University and National Bureau of Economic Research Working Paper (2015).

55. Massey, *Categorically Unequal.*

56. US Department of Labor, "Economic News Release: Union Members Summary," January 26, 2017, http://www.bls.gov/news.release/union2.nr0.htm.

57. Department for Business, Innovation and Skills, *Trade Union Membership 2012* (2013), http://www.gov.uk/government/uploads/system/uploads/attachment_data/file/204169/bis-13-p77-trade-union-membership-2012.pdf.

58. Stephen McFarland, " 'The Union Hall Was the Center of the Worker's Life': Spaces of Class Formation in the United Auto Workers, 1937–1970," *Journal of Historical Geography* 55 (2017): pp. 17–29.

59. Theriault, *The Unmaking of the American Working Class*, p. 7.

60. See White, *The Last Great Strike.*

61. Steve Early, *Save Our Unions: Dispatches from a Movement in Distress* (New York: Monthly Review Press, 2013), p. 25.

62. Aronowitz, *How Class Works*, pp. 15–16.

63. Rick Fantasia and Kim Voss, *Hard Work: Remaking the American Labor Movement* (Berkeley: University of California Press, 2004), pp. 26, 82–85.

64. Ibid., p. 85.
65. Martin Shefter, "Trade Unions and Political Machines: The Organization and Disorganization of the American Working Class in the Late Nineteenth Century," in *Working-Class Formation: Nineteenth-Century Patterns in Western Europe and the United States*, edited by Ira Katznelson and Aristide R. Zolberg (Princeton, NJ: Princeton University Press, 1986), pp. 197–276.
66. Rick Fantasia, *Cultures of Solidarity: Consciousness, Action, and Contemporary American Workers* (Berkeley: University of California Press, 1988).
67. Ibid.
68. Fantasia and Voss, *Hard Work*.
69. Ibid.
70. Ibid.
71. Early, *Save Our Unions*, pp. 26–27.
72. White, *The Last Great Strike*, pp. 29–30, 47.
73. "Economic News Release."
74. Justin Gest, *The New Minority: White Working Class Politics in an Age of Immigration and Inequality* (New York: Oxford University Press, 2016), pp. 47–48.
75. E. E. LeMasters, *Blue-Collar Aristocrats: Life-Styles at a Working-Class Tavern* (Madison: University of Wisconsin Press, 1975).
76. Michael Dennis, *Blood on Steel: Chicago Steelworkers and the Strike of 1937* (Baltimore, MD: Johns Hopkins University Press, 2014).
77. Some content in this section first appeared in *The American Prospect*. It is republished with permission.
78. Matt Grossmann and David A. Hopkins, *Asymmetric Politics: Ideological Republicans and Group Interest Democrats* (New York: Oxford University Press, 2016).
79. Kevin D. Williamson, "Chaos in the Family, Chaos in the State: The White Working Class's Dysfunction," *National Review*, March 17, 2016, http://www.nationalreview.com/article/432876/donald-trump-white-working-class-dysfunction-real-opportunity-needed-not-trump.

# INDEX

CPSIA information can be obtained
at www.ICGtesting.com
Printed in the USA
LVHW090856180120
644101LV00001B/153